TAKEN CARE OF

THE AUTOBIOGRAPHY OF

EDITH SITWELL

TAKEN CARE OF

THE AUTOBIOGRAPHY OF

EDITH SITWELL

ATHENEUM

NEW YORK

To

THE PERSONS FROM PORLOCK

*The publishers wish to acknowledge their
indebtedness to Miss Elizabeth Salter,
Dame Edith's secretary, whose help
throughout has been of the utmost value.*

Preface

This book was written under considerable difficulty. I had not recovered from a very severe and lengthy illness, which began with pneumonia. The infection from this permeated my body, and the bad poisoning of one finger lasted for fifteen months. This was agonisingly painful, and I could only use either hand with great difficulty, as the poison spread gradually.

The reminiscences in this book are of the past. I do not refer to any of my dearly loved living friends. I trust that I have hurt nobody. It is true that, provoked beyond endurance by their insults, I have given Mr. Percy Wyndham Lewis and Mr. D. H. Lawrence some sharp slaps. I have pointed out, also, the depths to which the criticism of poetry has fallen, and the non-nutritive quality of the bun-tough whinings of certain little poetasters—but I have been careful, for instance, not to refer to the late Mr. Edwin Muir (Dr. Leavis's spiritual twin-sister). I have attacked nobody unless they first attacked me.

During the writing of certain chapters of this book, I realised that the public would believe anything—so long as it is not founded on truth.

Edith Sitwell

Dame Edith Sitwell died on December 9, 1964, a short while after writing this preface.

Contents

Illustrations

TAKEN CARE OF

THE AUTOBIOGRAPHY OF

EDITH SITWELL

CHAPTER ONE

An Exceedingly Violent Child

Kierkegaard, in his *Journals*, wrote, "I am a Janus bifrons: I laugh with one face, I weep with the other."

In the following, but in no other way, do I resemble Savonarola, whose speech, though it related only to his home town and not the universe, was, unknown to me, the forerunner of mine.

A lady asked me why, on most occasions, I wore black. "Are you in mourning?"

"Yes."

"For whom are you in mourning?"

"For the world."

"You were an exceedingly violent child," said my mother, without any animus.

The summer of the year 1887 had been particularly hot. One afternoon in the first week of September, my grandparents, Lord and Lady Londesborough, or rather my grandmother (for my grandfather was a gentle creature whose motto seemed to be "laissez-faire") seized upon my mother's bedroom in Wood End, our house in Scarborough, as the field of one of the worst battles that even my grandmother had ever engendered. These two shadows—one tall and extremely dark (I knew a German governess who thought, when she saw him riding in Hyde Park, that he must be the Spanish Ambassador), one, my grandmother, like an effigy of the Plantagenet race, her ancestors—an effigy into which Rage, her Pygmalion, had breathed life—stood with their backs turned towards the window of the huge conservatory, a background of large tropical leaves and plants, from which, at moments, great flowers like birds flew into my mother's room.

This floriation had a strong period atmosphere: "silken cords, grey gauzes, green velvets, and crystal discs which blacken in the sun like gauze." *

My grandmother stormed, bringing about my early arrival into the world by this singularly appalling row. My beautiful eighteen-year-old mother, bored by the storm (there can have been, apart from the wars in which nations were involved, nothing to equal it before, or after, the San Francisco earthquake), lay in bed awaiting my birth. I, on my part, occupied my unborn

* "Fleurs," prose poem in Arthur Rimbaud's *Les Illuminations*, translated by Helen Rootham.

4

state with violent kickings and slappings against the walls of my prison, on the chance of my being let out. I did not know in what a world I was to find myself—in what a "siècle aux mains."

"I have wondered sometimes," my mother said, recalling this occasion, "whether this violence was because you were trying to be born, or whether you were wanting to get at your grandmother."

A short way from the house, the sea crawled like a lion awaiting its prey, so softly you could not guess of what tremendous roars that seemingly gentle creature was capable across the lion-yellow sands.

My grandmother's rage seemed to fill the universe.

For some time she had been surprised by the immense showers of emeralds, rivalling the splendour of the Niagara Falls, which descended upon her from jewellers at the request of my grandfather.

It was only on the day to which I refer that she discovered that he was in the habit of visiting ladies whom one might describe as the naiads sheltering behind those showers—nymphs who were occupied otherwise in prancing and squealing on the stage of musical comedies. After each of these visits, my grandfather was seized by remorse—hence the emeralds.

My grandmother said everything that came into her head. But she kept the emeralds.

On the 7th September, two days after this battle, my grandfather, who was President of the Scarborough Cricket Festival, gave a huge luncheon party on the cricket ground, in a tent decorated by flowering plants in tubs, and by the black beards, the eyebrows like branches of winter fir-trees, of Dr. W. G. Grace and other cricketers.

All went well until it became obvious to the assembled company that I was about to make my entry into the world. Narrowly escaping producing me on the cricket ground, my mother was rushed to Wood End, where, within the space of an hour or two, I was born.

I thought, once, that I remembered my birth. Perhaps what I remembered was my first experience of the light. In William James's *Principles of Psychology* he wrote, "The first time we see light, we *are* it rather than *see* it. But all our later knowledge is about what this experience gives: the first sensation an infant gets, is for him the universe."

That first sensation remains with every dedicated artist in all the arts. It has remained with me. "The infant," William James continued, "encounters an object in which all the categories of the understanding are contained. It has objectivity, causality, in the full sense in which any later object or system of objects have these things."

My parents understood nothing of what, from my childhood, was living in my head.

In an essay on an exhibition of Monsieur Masson's paintings, Monsieur André de Bouchet said, "While the painter's art was becoming acuter, . . . suns gave birth to innumerable other suns . . . a fierce sun vibrating over cock-fights, a butterfly sun vibrating over the painter's head, a bread sun behind the baker kneading her dough." All this I saw, transmuted from the painter's vision into the poet's. In a way, I had a wild beast's senses, a painter's eyesight. Artists in all the arts should have the eyes, the nose, of the lion, the lion's acuity of sense, and, with these, what Monsieur André Breton called "la construction solaire," the sun of man's reason.

But tall ghosts cast their shadows over my early, as on my later, life—ghosts tall as the wind of silence on the wall.

I do not wish to be cruel about a poor dead woman. I have forgiven the unhappiness long ago, and now write of it only because otherwise, after my death, much in me will be misunderstood. I now feel only pity for my mother, a poor young creature, married against her will into a kind of slave-bondage to an equally unfortunate and pitiable young man. Neither seems to have had the slightest knowledge of "the facts of life." My mother ran away a few days after the marriage and returned to her parents. But my grandmother sent her back. Changeling that I am, I was born nine months after that slavery began. No wonder that my mother hated me throughout my childhood and youth, though she became touchingly reconciled to me after disaster befell her— reconciled after a year in which she tried the worst kind of bullying, taking the form, mainly, of making the most horrible accusations against my moral character.

Then, suddenly, she forgave me for my existence. One night after this (I slept, at Renishaw, in the room next to hers), she called to me:

"Edith, have you ever been happy?"

"Yes, mother," I answered. "Haven't you?"

"Never *bird*-happy," she replied. "Still, I have three very nice children." Then, sighing, she went to sleep again.

My mother was a young woman of great beauty—Italianate in character. She bore a strong resemblance to one of the drawings by Michelangelo in the Uffizi Gallery, a drawing of a young woman of an extraordinary summer-like beauty, facing an old woman—herself grown old, but bearing still traces of that "high midsummer pomp," that majestic beauty.

At the same time, my mother bore a likeness to this great line describing the Furies: "The barren daughters of the fruitful night." Nothing was born in her head, which was barren; but my brothers and I were born of her fruitful night.

When young, she was very gay, was very generous, and lavished on others everything that belonged to her. She had a childlike quality. In later years, after she had fallen among thieves, her appearance still retained vestiges of that summer beauty, but as though a black veil had been thrown over it. Her hair was still dark as though it had lain under the shadow of a Fury's wing. She was still lavish, still wildly hospitable.

When at Montegufoni, she came to life and found gaiety in arranging those enormous luncheon and dinner parties to which she and my father succeeded, inevitably, in inviting deadly enemies to meet each other. But at Renishaw, deprived of those hours of hectic hospitality, Time was for her but an empty round between the night and night, a repetition of sad nothingness, like the beat that sounded within her dress of dust;

8

for her, the moments dropped like sad and meaningless tears.

Somehow she must cross the desert of her days, and that was all she knew. To her, all greatness was reduced to the smallness, the uselessness, of a grain of sand; those grains, the little things of life, without sense, without sap, were piled above her until she lay buried beneath them. "I live from day to day," she would reply in answer to enquiries as to her mode of life. She might have added, "and for the small distractions of the hour." Her rages were the only reality in her life.

While at Renishaw, she spent, invariably, her mornings in bed (so do I, but those mornings of mine are fully occupied)—and this she did because there was nothing to do if she got up. She lay there, also, because her feet, of which she was proud, hurt her, owing to the fact that she insisted on having her shoes made a size too small for her. Lying in bed, therefore, she read the newspapers; but even this was unprofitable to her, for when the end of the day came, she found that she could not remember one single fact recorded in them, or one phrase; and the same applied to novels, of which she was an omnivorous reader.

"Have I read that?" she would enquire, when a book was mentioned.

"I don't care *what* I am reading," she said, "as long as I *am* reading. It passes the time."

So she passed the nullity of her days, the blank stretch between hour and hour. She could not know oblivion, for there was always the hollow sound of Time, recalling her, not to herself, for she had no self, only a bundle of small griefs and fears, and mountainous furies—but to the fact that the days were passing, in a darkened and mournful procession towards the grave.

And on the wall behind her, the shadow of this light and inconsiderable being seemed larger than she, as if it was an effigy of ruin: the movements of that stupendous and sleepless shade had a furious quality, a quality of desperation, as if it prophesied doom.

In spite of her rages (the result of half-forgotten miseries, of disappointments), there were moments, just before the ambush into which she fell materialised, when she softened towards me—such moments as those when she planned the suppers for the Hospital Ball at Scarborough: "Of course, darling, we *must have* quails!" Or when, with a far-away, idealistic look in her eyes, she would say, "Of course, what I would *really* like would be to get your father put in a lunatic asylum."

My father's appearance in later life differed entirely from that which I remember in my earliest childhood. Then he was good-looking in an insipid way, the insipidity being largely the result of his blinking, with pink eyelids, if he was contradicted or came near to feeling shame—when he spoke about money, for instance, as on the occasion when I, being extremely poor, had earned £15 (then to me a large sum).

"I hope," he said to me, "you are saving up for the Little Men"—his grandsons. (Poor dear chivalrous creatures, the suggestion would have horrified them!)

I forget what I answered, but he remained silent, looking indescribably mean, as if he ought to have had a portrait painted of him (wearing two top hats, one on

10

top of the other, and a shabby fur-lined coat) posed against a shop-window bearing the device of three gilt balls.

In later life, he lost these attributes and became very handsome and noble-looking; with his strange, pale, wild, lonely-looking eyes, and his red beard, he resembled a portrait of one of the Borgias, or some other early Italian tyrant.

Of course, my father's principal worry was my mother, who had an objectionable habit of indulging in gaieties. When she died, dear old Henry Moat, my father's valet and my brothers' and my lifelong friend, said, "Well, at least Sir George will know now where Her Ladyship spends her afternoons."

My father was extremely active physically, and he had adopted, in later life, the custom of pacing the long passages at Renishaw because, he said, by cultivating such a habit one ceased to trouble if the days were wet and cold, or torrid and weighted by the heat, were drawing out or drawing in. If you paid no attention to a fact, it ceased to exist. He remembered, however, that the weather was useful as a basis for conversation (he would speak with approbation of noisy female non-entities who "kept the ball rolling," by which he meant rattling out unceasing nonsense obliterating the passage of time, at every meal). Apart from these interludes, only the sound of his footsteps and the care for his health remained to bind him to reality. He did not believe in taking risks, however, and, though an agnostic by profession, said his prayers every night, on the chance of this being a good investment.

When pacing the passages he walked very slowly, occupying as much time as possible, in order that the house should seem even larger than it is—for he liked to think of it as very large. Occasionally (about once or twice a day) he would pause outside a door, if he could hear voices in the room beyond—not because he wanted to eavesdrop or to spy, since there was nothing he could hear that would interest him, but because he was enabled in this way to touch, for a moment, the world in which others moved, thought, acted, without being obliged to become part of it; and this made him real to himself, real in his isolation, in the separation of his identity from the world that he could yet touch at will. For this reason he would pretend to secret information from an unknown source: "We happen to know," he would say; and when a letter arrived for my mother in a handwriting he did not know, he would enquire "How are *they*?" He would spread various objects belonging to himself all over the house, in the many rooms—his hat in one room, his stick in another, his spectacle case in a third—because when he came face to face once more, in the course of his wanderings, with these records of his personality, he was reminded of himself, which was pleasant, and because it enabled him to stake his claim on every room in the house as sole inhabitant. Should any other person enter one of the rooms in question, my father would follow him there, and, conveying suddenly the impression of very great age, would make it clear by his manner that he had intended to rest there and had hoped that he would not be disturbed. Then, having by this means routed the intruder and put him to flight, he would continue his walk.

When he was not pacing up and down the passages, my father spent much of his time in walking up and down outside the house, and when he did this, he would succeed in appearing like a procession of one person—he being the head, the beginning and the end.

You were conscious of the State Umbrella. On these occasions he would begin by walking rather fast, and briskly, with what seemed to be determination; but it was noticeable that his left foot turned inward towards the right, as if seeking reassurance; and after a while it became apparent that he was going nowhere in particular; he seemed to be walking solely because he wished to feel the earth solid beneath him. He rarely spoke to the members of his family, or to visitors, seeming, indeed, to be separated from them by an endless plain—a stretch of centuries, perhaps, a continent with all its differences of climate, or the enormous space that divides these. Occasionally, however, a gesture or wave of the hand, a smile of great kindliness would be flashed across the plain, from planet to earth. And he had a habit of talking to himself, if not to others, muttering phrases in an unused voice: "They may *think* I shall, but I *shan't!*" Or, with his head a little on one side, he would whisper down to a confidential shoulder: "And if *they* do that, then *I* shall take the opposite direction." And, having said this, he would, once in a while, give a queer, rusty, creaking laugh, whose sound was that of a gate that had been shut for so long that it was difficult for it to move upon its hinges, more difficult still for it to open wide. Having laughed, he would take out his watch and look at it shamefacedly, although Time meant nothing to him. So he continued, walking up and down with a sound like the beat of Time in an empty house, a sound like the drip of rain falling from the leaves, echoing through the house. When not pacing up and down, he meditated on various abstruse theories. He took, for instance, a great (but disapproving) interest in Einstein's Theory of Relativity, which he professed to understand; and he had numerous theories of his own—mainly dotty—about one thing or another.

Apart from the fact that he had married my mother, my father's principal worry was that the world did not understand that it had been created in order to prove his theories. Like one of the characters in *Lavengro*, he could have said: "The world must exist in order to have the shape of a pear. And that the world is shaped like a pear, and not like an apple as certain fools say, I have satisfactorily proved. Now, if there were no world, what would become of my system?"

CHAPTER TWO

In Disgrace for Being a Female

I was unpopular with my parents from the moment of my birth, and throughout my childhood and youth. I was in disgrace for being a female, and, worse, as I grew older it was obvious that I was not going to conform to my father's standard of feminine beauty. I in no way resembled a Pekinese, or one of those bloated pink imitation roses that my father (who had never forgiven himself for marrying a lady) admired. Instead, I had inherited the Plantagenet features and deep-set eyes of my grandmother Londesborough.

My parents were displeased with me, for they would have liked such a child as that born to a woman called Mary Clark in 1788: "It appeared to the doctors that her head presented a curious appearance." But this curiosity "did not trouble the doctors much, for the child behaved in the usual manner, and it was not until the evidence of its death became undeniable . . . that it

was realised there was not the least indication of either
cerebrum, cerebellum, or any medullary substance
whatever." This would have been an ideal child. But,
alas, I have never behaved in the usual manner, nor
could it be denied, even at the earliest age, that I showed
strong indications of cerebrum, cerebellum and medullary substance. I was a disappointment. My eighteen-
year-old mother had thought she was being endowed
with a new doll—one that would open and shut its eyes
at her bidding and say "Papa," "Mama." I was unsatis-
factory in those ways, as in every other.

My father had only one comfort. In my earliest childhood, before he had retired into a Trappist seclusion
within himself, he had seen himself always as the apex
of one of those hierarchical family pyramids favoured
by photographers. Then, when I was just able to walk,
he saw this imaginary photograph labelled "Charming
photograph of a young father with his child." And,
under the spell of this fantasy, he would bowl me over
with a cushion, pinning my forehead to the iron fender.

My parents were strangers to me from the moment of
my birth.

I do not forget that I must have been a most ex-
asperating child, living with violence each moment of
my day. I was rather a fat little girl: my moon-round
face, which was surrounded by green-gold curls, had,
strangely for so small a child—indeed, for any child—
the eyes of someone who had witnessed and foretold all
the tragedy of the world. Perhaps I, at four years old,
knew the incipient anguish of the poet I was to become.

Yet in my earliest childhood, when not being bullied,

I was ineffably happy under those strange suns that illumined only *my* life and were unknown by others—by the children who seemed of another race and who could not play with me. (The children's parties to which I was driven were an agony to me. The children wanted to be kind to me, but could not because I was a foreigner. I was known, always, as "poor little E." I did not regard myself as superior to them—I have never, in all my life, been so odious as to regard myself as "superior" to any living being, human or animal. I just walked alone—as I have always walked alone.) But I had not yet reached those years of my later childhood when, like Arthur Rimbaud (in some ways my closest spiritual relation), I could say, as he said in *Une Saison en Enfer*, "Une voix étreignait mon coeur gelé. . . . On ne te tuera pas plus que si tu étais cadavre! . . . Au matin j'avais le regard si perdu et la contenance si morte, que ceux que j'ai rencontrés *ne m'ont peut-être pas vu*."

My friends were my dear old nurse, Davis (when I think of her now, I see her like a phrase in my friend Gertrude Stein's *Geography and Plays:* "A shadow, a white shadow, is a mountain." She was at once a white shadow and a mountain. And her real name was comfort), and my father's valet, Henry Moat, whose friendship with my brothers and me lasted until his death. (On the night of his death—or rather just before the light dawned—Osbert heard that far-away friend, lying on his deathbed at Whitby, moving about in the pantry at Renishaw that had been for so long his home. I believe—I like to think—that he was looking for the three children, now two grown men and a grown

17

woman, whom he had befriended through the sad
years.) I think of him as if at any moment his living
being might come through a door and say to me, "You'd
better run, Miss Edith. Her Ladyship is in one of her
states and is looking for you." He was an enormous
purple man like a benevolent hippopotamus, and had a
voice like some foghorn endowed with splendour. He
had eighteen brothers, all as large and strong as himself, and one sister. They came of a long line of whaling
captains dating from the time of Queen Elizabeth the
First.

I have referred already to the fact that my father saw
himself, always, as the centre of a photograph. I must
have been a very small child when he decided to be
immortalised, together with his family, in drawings or
paintings by artists who under no circumstances could
be regarded as dangerous. (The pictorial art was, to
him, a means of dwarfing and distorting reality—not
heightening it, as is the unfortunate habit of great
artists.) I remember one drawing purporting to repre-
sent my grandmother Sitwell, my Aunt Florence with
her gilded wilderness of hair firmly restrained, and my
father, having tea in the conservatory at Wood End.
They were surrounded by a multitude of very fussy
shapeless leaves. The silver teapot and kettle were
drawn with respect, if not awe, and had more an appearance of reality than the three human beings represented.
My father was dressed as a cricketer and was carrying a
bat. He never played cricket, but it was obvious from the
drawing that he was, for some reason, inseparable from
the bat, and that he had just returned from a match in

18

which the triumph was his alone—the rest of the eleven being but figments of the imagination.

There was also a pretty portrait of my mother dressed in light blue and white, and with her lazy hands resting on the strings of a zither. (She had never played a zither.)

I had, I regret to say, inherited my grandmother Londesborough's violent temper—but not her passion for making rows about trivial subjects. I did not like being thwarted, however, and remember an occasion on which I was travelling to London but had to be taken back to Scarborough in disgrace because, owing to a rival train passing ours, I yelled with frustration.

I was an embarrassing child. There was an occasion when Davis was asked to bring me down to the drawing-room at Wood End to see one of mother's friends, a delightful young woman with a summery appearance. She was thin-waisted like a Minoan bee-priestess. She cast a shadow like a long bird. It seemed as if it must be singing, and had nothing to do with the darkness of grief. Poor Rita! Some years after this time, worn out by poverty and a hopeless love affair, she killed herself.

"You remember me, little E?" she enquired when I was brought into the room. (For some reason, I was always addressed by this one letter, until my brother Osbert, at that time unborn, was able to speak. Then I was called "Dish" as it was impossible for his baby tongue to pronounce "Edith.")

"Don't you remember me?"

"No."

"Children have the most unreliable memory," said

my father, blinking.

"What are you going to be when you are grown-up, little E?" asked Rita, a warm-hearted creature who wished to avert from me my parents' wrath.

"A genius," I replied.

I was promptly removed from the drawing-room and put to bed. But my disgrace was not forgotten, and was frequently referred to, in after years, in a disgusted whisper.

There was another unfortunate scene in my grandmother Londesborough's bedroom, when her wrinkles were being dusted over by her maid with a heliotrope-coloured powder.

"Granny, why do you have your face turned that mauve colour?"

"Because it makes Granny look pretty, darling."

"Oh no, it doesn't. Oh no, it doesn't."

"Miss E, you naughty girl. How dare you speak to Her Ladyship like that? I shall take you back to the nursery."

"No, don't take the child away. I like having her here."

"Then, Granny, as it doesn't make you look pretty, why do you have it that colour?"

"Because poor Granny has a dreadful headache."

"Then E will sing to you and make it better."

Whereupon I burst into song—my own version of the hymn "We plough the fields and scatter"—and was removed from circulation, as it was thought I had gone too far.

My grandmother seems to have borne me no malice,

for I remember, soon after, staying with my grandparents in a house they had in the New Forest—and
standing under a huge flowering magnolia tree, talking
to Macpherson the gardener, who was . . .

old as tongues of nightingales
That in the wide leaves tell a thousand Grecian tales

. . . the ancient man, wrinkled like old moonlight
Beneath dark boughs. . . .

And I remember, too, driving every afternoon with
my great-grandmother, the very aged Dowager Duchess of Beaufort, the original of the Dowager Queen
in my poem "The Sleeping Beauty" and of the old
woman in "Colonel Fantock." She looked as if, at any
moment, she would crumble into a little silvery dust.
She never discovered—nodding into a sleep that would
soon be eternal—that we drove on the same route every
afternoon.

At about this time my grandfather suffered from
periodic attacks of gout, and to soothe the feelings of
what must undoubtedly have been the savage breast, my
grandmother would cause her daughters Lily and Mil-
dred to play on the piano duets of melodies from the
latest musical comedies. Both ladies had hands of an
extraordinary beauty, but they were not pianists' hands,
and although they played correctly, the sound was
reminiscent of "Hen's hooves hitting the hard high
road."

* * *

I wondered, sometimes, if the sound *did* soothe the savage breast. I myself was, at this early age, inexorably sick, regardless of any company in which I found myself, if victimised by any music which offended me. (There was one terrible song, for instance, "Queen of My Heart," which brought on this expression of disapproval. And years later, when I was twelve years old, I was publicly sick in the Albert Hall during a performance of "The Washington Post" by the late Mr. Sousa's exuberant but strongly tailored band.)

My first real adventure, outside those which even then illuminated my mind, was my visit to Cannes, when I was four years old (Osbert was as yet unborn). Of the sea journey I remember only the elephant-like trumpeting of the sirens, and my incessant shrieks because the ship, with unaccountable obstinacy, continued its course without asking my permission.

The train journey was fraught with danger. My mother occupied the lower berth of our sleeping compartment, while Davis and I, by means of a very rickety ladder, climbed to the upper berth. I was suffering from a stye on one of my eyes, and howled most dismally. My mother, never slow to wrath (and certainly on this occasion she deserved every sympathy), threatened to throw me out of the window. This project, throughout my early childhood, was her method of inducing affection. I howled, of course, even more loudly.

I was not thrown out, otherwise this record would never have been written; and Davis soothed my mother by making tea in an upper berth, endangering, by means of a flaring spirit-lamp and spluttering matches, the train, ourselves, and our fellow travellers.

However, in spite of these dangers, we arrived, to find ourselves in a world where flowers reigned, with their scent like a soul, in great fields of narcissi that seemed white shadows cast by the snow-covered mountains above them, and fields of yellow jonquils that, in my later life, were like the spirits of my early poetry:

Jonquilles, dont on fit les cils de tant de blondes filles,

Narcisse oriental, fleur inféconde et pas morale,

Soucis dorés, charme effaré du familier succube étoile errante, flamme dans les cheveux tristes du pauvre Songe,

Jonquille, Narcisse et soucis, je vous préfère
Aux plus claires chevelures, fleurs trepassées,
fleurs de janis.

So wrote poor Remy de Gourmont, seeing that beauty in spite of the tragic disease that had partially destroyed his face. And that lovely passage remains with me like a memory of those fields in which I walked as a little child (although there were, in that springtime, no soucis dorés, no marigolds).

One day, in those fields, as Davis and I were standing under the pale green light, that was like water flowing, of an eucalyptus tree, she said to me, "*Her* carriage is coming. You must curtsey."

The barouche contained an old lady in widow's

weeds. I curtseyed, and received an impressive bow.

The old lady was Queen Victoria. I was curtseying to an age, a world, that was passing.

On our return to Renishaw, I concentrated my love on the Renishaw peacock. This love was, at the time, returned.

When we were at Renishaw, punctually at nine o'clock every morning (it is strange how birds and animals have an accurate sense of time) the peacock would stand on leads outside my mother's bedroom, waiting for me to come and say good morning to her. When he saw me, he would utter a harsh shriek of welcome (I do not, as a rule, appreciate ugly voices, but I loved him so much that nothing about him could be wrong, in my opinion). He would wait for me until I left my mother's room, then, with another harsh shriek, would fly down into the large gardens. We walked round these, with my arm round his lovely neck, that shone like tears in a dark forest. If it had not been for his crown, which made him slightly taller than me, we should have been of the same height.

Davis said to me, "Why do you love Peaky so much?"

I said, "Because he is beautiful and wears a Heavenly Crown."

("The pride of the peacock," said William Blake, "is the Glory of God.")

This romance lasted for months. Then my father bought Peaky a wife (in my eyes a most dull and insignificant bird) and he discarded my companionship and devoted himself entirely to teaching his children to unfurl the tails with which they had been endowed as fans.

I do not think it was the injury to my pride at being jilted by a peacock that I minded. It was the injury to my affection. It was my first experience of faithlessness. My other friends at this time were a puffin with a wooden leg (his real leg had been injured in an accident: he was like an old sea-captain from some book by Dickens) and a baby owl that had fallen out of its nest, and which used to sleep with its head on my shoulder, pretending to snore in order to attract mice. But until the birth of Osbert, when I was five years old, my only human friends, apart from Davis, Henry Moat, and my cousin Veronica, daughter of my aunt Sybil Codrington, were Mollie and Gladys Hume, the daughters of a Colonel Hume, a tall stork-like personage who resembled a character in *Struwwelpeter*. (One imagined him, always, as carrying a gun, stalking over green baize grass against a background of large leaves of the same colour and texture, a fleeing hare—or like a character in Mr. Stravinsky's *Chansons Plaisantes*. Both these works have influenced, very greatly, my early poetry.)

Colonel Hume was the original of Old Sir Faulk in my "Fox Trot"—as far as his physique was concerned. But I placed him in the countryside of our dear old friend and neighbour Colonel Chandos-Pole, at Radburne.

The Hume children were of about the same age as myself, four or five. One afternoon, after I had not seen

them for some time, Davis and I went to tea with them.
They seemed little shadowed beings, dressed in black.
Their mother was generally present at nursery tea, but
on this occasion she was not there, and I asked where
she was. They cried bitterly. "She is dead," they said.
Soon afterwards we left, not staying for the usual after-
teatime games. I asked Davis why they had cried.

"Because their mother is dead."

"Yes, I know. But why did they *cry?*"

Old
> *Sir*
>> *Faulk,*
>> *Tall as a stork,*

*Before the honeyed fruits of dawn were ripe, would
    walk*
And stalk with a gun
The reynard-coloured sun,
*Among the pheasant-feathered corn the unicorn has
    torn, forlorn the*
Smock-faced sheep
Sit
> *And*
>> *Sleep;*

Periwigged as William and Mary, weep . . .
"Sally, Mary, Mattie, what's the matter, why cry?"
*The huntsman and the reynard-coloured sun and I
    sigh;*
"Oh, the nursery-maid Meg
With a leg like a peg

26

Chased the feathered dreams like hens, and when they
  laid an egg
In the sheepskin
Meadows
Where
The serene King James would steer
Horse and Hounds, then he
From the shade of a tree
Picked it up as spoil to boil for nursery tea," said the
  mourners. In the
Corn, towers strain,
Feathered tall as a crane,
And whistling down the feathered rain, old Noah goes
  again—
An old dull mome
With a head like a pome,
Seeing the world as a bare egg
Laid by the feathered air; Meg
Would beg three of these
For the nursery teas
Of Japhet, Shem, and Ham; she gave it
Underneath the trees,
Where the boiling
          Water,
            Hissed,
Like the goose-king's feathered daughter—kissed
Pot and pan and copper kettle
Put upon their proper mettle,
Lest the Flood—the Flood—the Flood begin again
  through these!

27

This poem, as other of my early poems, was, to quote Monsieur Jean Cocteau on another subject, "the poetry of childhood overtaken by a technician."

It is an experiment in the effect, on rhythm and on speed, of certain arrangements of assonances and dissonances, and of a certain arrangement of intertwining one-syllabled, two-syllabled, and three-syllabled words.

The ground-rhythm of the beginning of this poem is partly the result of the drone-sounds in the first lines, the dissonances, so subtle they might almost be assonances, of "Faulk," "tall," "stork," "before," "walk," each having a different depth of darkness, "tall" and the second syllable of "before" for instance, while the sounds differ (though with an almost incredible faintness) both in darkness and in length, dip much deeper in both cases than "Faulk" or "stork," while the sound of "stork" is slightly darker than "Faulk."

All these drone-sounds seem pleasant country shadows, varying slightly in depth, in warmth, in length. In the fifth and seventh lines, the words "honeyed" and "reynard" are a little rounder than "pheasant-feathered," and each casts a little dipping, reversed shadow, because the light, fleeting character of the second syllable of "honeyed" suddenly grows dark in its dissonance, the second syllable of "reynard," while the first syllable of "honeyed" is a faintly darker dissonance of the "rey" of "reynard." The shadows, therefore, fall in opposite directions.

The fact that in the line

The reynard-coloured sun

(reynard-coloured—the fox-coloured sun of early autumn) the words ending in the letter D are placed so close together makes, in this particular case, a slight leap into the air, while, some lines farther on, the three-syllabled words of:

> *Periwigged as William and Mary, weep . . .*

twirl round on themselves: and the assonances, placed in such juxtaposition, of

> *Among the pheasant-feathered corn the unicorn has*
> *torn, forlorn the*

gives a particular smoothness; the line might consist of one word only were it not for the change from sunniness to darkness.

The Ea sounds, on which much of the poem is based, vary in lightness; at moments the effect is of light pleasant stretches of cornfields, as in:

> *Among the pheasant-feathered corn the unicorn has*
> *torn, forlorn the*

over which the flying shadows of the darker-vowelled "corn," "unicorn," "torn," "forlorn," dip and are gone.

In the line

> *"Sally, Mary, Mattie, what's the matter, why cry?"*

the changing of the assonances, from the limpness of "Sally" to the hardness of "Mattie," the reversal of sound in the second syllables, from "Mattie" to "matter"—these have a very faint effect upon the rhythm, while the exact rhymes "why cry," placed together, give a high leap into the air. Throughout the poem the assonances and dissonances are placed in a closely concerted and interwoven design, some being accented and some so unaccented as to be almost muted; they are largely responsible for the rhythm, and often counterpoint it slightly, as in

Oh, the nursery-maid Meg
With a leg like a peg
Chased *the feathered dreams like hens, and when they*
    laid an egg

where the high A sounds counterpoint, the "Meg," "leg," "peg," "egg" round off the ground-rhythm.

These A or Ai sounds are echoed, farther on in the poem, more insistently, and with a deeper emphasis, by

            In the
Corn, towers strain,
Feathered tall as a crane,
And whistling down the feathered rain, *old Noah*
    goes again—

where these assonances, while they are slightly counterpointed, are yet nearly as important as the ground-rhythm given by "corn" and "tall."

It will be seen how slack is the rhythm, in comparison with the rest, of such lines as have only an end rhyme and no apparent assonances or dissonances, as in the second line of

            An old dull mome
            With a head like a pome

30

Though "head" is immediately linked up again in the next line with "egg," yet because it had no previous related sound, there is no effect on rhythm.

A faint and fleeting country shadow is cast again, later in the poem, by the changing of the "aph" in "Japhet" to the dimmer V of "gave" in the lines

> *Of Japhet, Shem and Ham; she gave it*
> *Underneath the trees.*

CHAPTER THREE

The Sound of Poetry

My childhood, when I was not being bullied by my mother, resembled, before the birth of my two much-loved brothers, that of the child in Rimbaud's "Enfance" (I was an arrogant young being) who had "neither family nor courtiers. . . . The staring azure and greenery which is her kingdom runs along level shores which the shipless waves have called by names ferociously Greek, Slav, and Celtic.

"On the forest-verge, where dream-flowers tinkle, glitter, and shine, sits the young girl, clothed by the passing shadows of the rainbows, by the shadows of the flowers and sea."

This was my inner life when I was a child of, say, twelve—it was then untouched by the brutish outer life in which my outer world was extinguished.

"The Species of Visibles," wrote my collateral ancestor Francis Bacon, in his *Naturall History*, "seem to be *Emissions of Beames* from the Object seen, almost like Odours, save that they are more Incorporate."

So should be the sound of poetry. And from my earliest age, these Emissions of Beames came to me from all the objects I saw.

Al was this land fulfild of faëry.

I learned to read before I was four years old, my reading then consisting of the fairy tales of the Brothers Grimm and Hans Andersen. Many stories of the latter frightened me, as I could not bear the loneliness that seemed to pervade them. I shrank from the coldness of the Snow Queen. Now my life is warm, but when I was a child I was ineffably cold and lonely. So much so that I ran away from home when I was five years old (I do not know to what I was escaping)—but as I could not do up my buttoned boots and had no money, I was captured by a young policeman and restored to my parents. (By that time Osbert had been born, but that warm heart that has never failed anyone could not, as he was only a few weeks old, find speech to express itself.)

But there was another, ugly, commonplace world to be faced.

My friend the baby owl, as we have seen in a previous chapter, had to snore in order to attract the attention of mice. Throughout my life, I have been so unfortunate as to attract mice (of the human species) without the effort of snoring.

By the time I was eleven years old, I had been taught that Nature, far from abhorring a Vacuum, positively adores it.

At about that time I was subjected, in the schoolroom, to a devoted, loving, peering, inquisitive, interfering, stultifying, middle-class suffocation, on the chance that I would become "just like everybody else."

Trotsky (in *Problems of Life*, translated by Z. Vervora) said, "It is well to have life ground by the grinders of proletarian thought. The grinders are strong, and will master anything they are given to grind."

The middle-class grinders to which I was, as a child, subjected in the schoolroom, and the grinders of upper-class mentality to which I was given over when a very young woman, have been attempting to subdue me throughout my life. They have never mastered me. The idea that I could be mastered by anyone or anything (of course my loving tormentors, in their proud edifices of cotton wool, have never been, even vaguely, in touch with proletarian thought) was simply the effect of wishful thinking.

In the midst of the suffocation to which I have referred, my parents noticed that I stooped slightly, owing to curvature of the spine, and that my very thin ankles were weak. I was therefore handed over, lock, stock, and barrel, to an orthopaedic surgeon in London, Mr. Stout. This gentleman's life consisted in one long campaign against the human frame. He decided, immediately, that I was all wrong from A to Z, and that my muscles must be atrophied as far as possible.

I remember little of Mr. Stout's outward appearance, excepting that he looked like a statuette constructed of margarine, then frozen so stiff that no warmth, either from the outer world or human feeling, could begin to melt it. The statuette was then swaddled in padded wool, to give an impression of burliness.

34

After my first interview with Mr. Stout, I was trundled off to an orthopaedic manufacturer and incarcerated in a sort of Bastille of steel. This imprisonment began under my arms, preventing me from resting them on my sides. My legs were also imprisoned down to my ankles, and at night-time these, and the soles of my feet, were locked up in an excruciating contraption. Even my nose did not escape this gentleman's efficiency, and a band of elastic surrounded my forehead, from which two pieces of steel (regulated by a lock-and-key system) descended on each side of the organ in question, with thick upholstered pads at the nostrils, turning my nose very firmly to the opposite way which Nature had intended, and blocking one nostril, so that breathing was difficult. This *latter* adornment, however, was only worn during my long hours in the schoolroom, as it was thought that it might arouse some speculation—even, perhaps, indignation—in passers-by if worn in the outer world.

I mention this Bastille existence of my childhood only because it throws a light on my later life, having semi-atrophied the muscles of my back and legs. For some reason, my hands and arms remained in freedom, so that I am able to move these with, I might even say, fluidity of motion, expressiveness.

The manufacturer of my Bastille, Mr. Steinberg, was an immensely fat gentleman who seemed to spread over London like a fog. This impression was enhanced by the fact that he was fog-yellow. His eyes, and all the expression that they may have held, were shrouded behind black glasses.

Long after my childhood was over, I came face to face, once again, with those black and airless dummy windows, in an omnibus in Bayswater, and felt again the sickened fright, humiliation, and sense of hopeless imprisonment I had known as a child.

My parents were surrounded, for the most part, by semi-animate persons like an unpleasant form of vegetation, or like dolls confected out of cheap satin, with, here and there, buttons fastened on their faces in imitation of eyes.

My mother was slightly too insistent on her social position (those were the days when an Earl was regarded as a being on the highest mountain peaks, to be venerated, but not approached, by ordinary mortals). She was in the habit of saying (no doubt with my father in mind), "A Baronet is the lowest thing on God's earth"—lower, presumably, than a black beetle. And when she was in a rage with me—this being a constant state with her—she would say to me, "*I* am better-born than *you* are." This puzzled me slightly.

But my mother's insistence on her social position did not prevent her from making close friends with persons who could not possibly have found their way into Lady Londesborough's drawing-room.

One of the worst of these sub-humans was Miss Diana Pilkington, an alleged beauty. She was a person who seemed to have been divided exactly in two. The upper part of her body consisted of an enormous pink ham which served her as face. The lower half was like one of those legless toys which rock from side to side if given a slight push.

36

She was a thick dulled creature behind that great inexpressive pink façade, which had blunt unformed features affixed to it simply because she had to have a mouth with which to eat, and a nose with which to smell out the miseries of others.

The occupation of trying to attract admiration filled up, for the most part, her days, although her coarse pink fingers, that looked as if someone had cut them off, like meat, at the first joints, would sometimes indulge in "ribbon-work"—sewing imitation pink and scarlet Dorothy Perkins roses of bunched ribbons on to obstreperously shiny white satin (needlework which had recently been imitated from one of the more stupid eighteenth-century minor painters).

Though she was of *completely contemporary human* origin, she yet aroused in me the conjecture that the Almighty had been trying on her His 'prentice Hand.

She had a shocking influence on my mother, who seemed to be entirely hypnotised by her commonness. (My mother, at that time, had but few companions. They came, but either the wind from the North Sea, or some aimless, dull, spiritual wind, blew them away again.)

On a few occasions Miss Pilkington induced my mother to accompany her on a midnight rat-hunt in the cellars of a large hotel in Scarborough. (This was Miss Pilkington's preferred sport. But it was a strange behaviour for a woman of my mother's breeding and fastidious cleanliness. She was, as I have said, hypnotised.)

Rat-catchers, terriers, and large sticks would be collected, and Miss Pilkington would join the rat-catchers in knocking the squealing creatures on the head, and encouraging the terriers to worry their throats. Spattered with rat blood, "The best fun in the world," she would say.

Diana Pilkington enjoyed watching suffering. It was an especial joy to her to intrude into my schoolroom, in order to feast herself on the humiliation I suffered in my Bastille of steel. Often she would bring with her persons of an equal breeding, complete strangers to me, and they would laugh openly and delightedly at my helpless state.

My grandmother Londesborough was kept in ignorance of the existence of this dreadful woman and "the best fun in the world." "I am afraid I shall not be able to see you and your sisters while my mother is in Scarborough," they were told!

Every Saturday afternoon I was "kept in" as a punishment, because I either could not, or would not, learn by heart "The Boy Stood on the Burning Deck," the Boy in question being, in my childish eyes, the epitome of idiocy, because, as everybody else had left the Burning Deck and he was doing no conceivable good by remaining there, why in heck didn't he get off it! I was unwilling, therefore, to pay lip-service to this idiotic episode.

This refusal, on my part, was recurrent when I was between the ages of eleven and thirteen.

On the other hand, I knew the whole of Pope's "The

Rape of the Lock"—the only poem of genius to be found at Wood End—before I was thirteen (having learned it secretly at night when my governess was at dinner— sitting up in bed, bending over it, poring over it).

From the thin, glittering, occasionally shadowed, airy, ever varying texture of that miracle of poetry, the instinct was instilled into me that not only structure, but also texture, are parents of rhythm in poetry, and that variations in speed are the result, not only of structure, but also of texture.

I was to learn, in after life, that the ineffably subtle and exquisite changes in the following lines, for instance, from a passage about the Sylphs

Some to the Sun their Insect-Wings unfold,
Waft on the Breeze, or sink in Clouds of gold;
Transparent Forms, too fine for mortal sight,
Their fluid Bodies half dissolv'd in Light.
Loose to the Wind their airy Garments flew,
Thin, glitt'ring Textures of the filmy Dew,
Dipt in the richest Tincture of the Skies,
Where Light disports in ever-mingling Dyes,
While ev'ry Beam new transient Colours flings,
Colours that change whene'er they wave their Wings

are caused by particular arrangements of one-syllabled and two-syllabled words with others that have the slightest possible fraction of an extra syllable, casting a tiny shadow or, when placed close together, producing a faint stretching pause—as with "their airy" (here, of course, the fact that these words are assonances adds to the effect). The changes in the movement are caused, also, by softening assonances, such as "some," "sun," placed in a certain arrangement with assonances that change from softness to poignancy—"Insect-Wings," "Thin, glitt'ring" (the poignancy of the G in "Wings" lengthens the line very slightly). The changes in the movement are caused, also, by an incredibly subtle and ever varying arrangement of alliteration and of vowel-schemes, these latter stretching the line, making it wave in the air, heightening it or letting it sink.

But in discussing this, of course, I speak as a practised poet, not as the child in whom this knowledge began as instinct.

I do not intend to write more about my schoolroom days. I learned from the world, not from maps. And all living beings, human, animal, or plants, were my brothers.

To me, as a child, glory was everywhere, and what visited me then, in my sleep, visits my working world now that I am a woman.

Ever since my earliest childhood, seeing the immense design of the world, one image of wonder mirrored by another image of wonder—the pattern of fur and feather by the frost on the windowpane, the six rays of the snowflake mirrored in the rock-crystal's six-rayed eternity—seeing the pattern on the scaly legs of birds mirrored in the pattern of knot-grass, I asked myself, were those shapes moulded by blindness? These were the patterns used by me, consciously or unconsciously, in certain of my early poems, *Bucolic Comedies*.

In many of my early poems the subject is the growth of consciousness. Sometimes it is like that of a person who has always been blind and who, suddenly endowed with sight, must *learn* to see; or it is the cry of that waiting, watching world, where everything we see is a symbol of something beyond, to the consciousness that is yet buried in this earth sleep.

The poem "Aubade," in its present state (having passed through my own life, my own experience), is about a country girl, a servant on a farm, plain, neglected and unhappy, with a bucolic stupidity, coming down in the dawn to light the fire.

The reason I said "The morning light creaks" is this: After rain, the early light seems as if it does not run quite smoothly. Also, it has a quality of great hardness and seems to present a physical obstacle to the shadows —and this gives one the impression of a creaking sound because it is at once hard and uncertain.

> *Each dull blunt wooden stalactite*
> *Of rain creaks, hardened by the light,*
>
> *Sounding like an overtone*
> *From some lonely world unknown.*

At dawn, long raindrops hanging from boughs seem transformed by the light, have the dull, blunt, tasteless quality of wood; though the sound is unheard in reality, it has the quality of an overtone from some unknown and mysterious world.

The lines

But the creaking empty light
Will never harden into sight,

Will never penetrate your brain
With overtones like the blunt rain

mean that to this girl, leaving her bed at dawn, the light is an empty thing which conveys nothing. It cannot bring her sight, because she is not capable of seeing.

In the kitchen you must light
Flames as staring, red and white,

As carrots or as turnips, shining
Where the cold dawn light lies whining.

To me, the shivering movement of a certain cold dawn light upon the floor suggests a kind of high animal whining or whimpering, a half-frightened and sub-servient urge to something outside our consciousness.

The poet must necessarily occupy himself, through all his life, in examining the meaning of material phe-nomena, and attempting to see what they reveal of the spiritual world. So I lived in my green world of growth, companioned by the animals and the plants.

That great mystic and philosopher Lorenz Oken wrote: "As the animal contains all elements in itself, so also it contains the plant, and is therefore both vegetable and animal kingdom, on the whole solar system.

"Animals are entire heavenly bodies, satellites or moons, which circulate independently about the earth; all plants, on the contrary, taken together, are only

42

equivalent to one heavenly body. An animal is an infinity of plants."

This was how I saw the world as a child, as I see it now, when I am allowed to see anything, for I am positively *hag-ridden*. Because I am a poet, it is assumed that I must wish to pass my life listening to conversations strayed from *Mrs. Dale's Diary*. Oddly enough, I do not. When I can escape from such excitements, I remember how Harvey—I quote this from A. J. Snow's *Matter and Gravity in Newton's Philosophy*—"thought that the heat in animals, which is not fire, and does not take its origin from fire, derives its origin from the solar ray." And I feel, humbly, that even *my* blood must derive from that ray.

It will not be believed by what a French critic called "Les Apôtres du Petit Bonheur," but the experience of the poet during the first inception and creation of a poem (here I am speaking of a poet in full command of his craft, not of a poet slowly finding his way) is akin—I say this with all humility—to the experience of the saint—but of a saint who has not yet shed all the trappings of earth.

"The Word," wrote St. Bernard (*Cantico*, Sermon 74), "has sprung in me more than once: if It has entered frequently, I have not always been conscious of Its arrival. But I have felt even the forerunning of Its entry.

"Whence did It enter my soul? Whence did It return on leaving me? What is the place of Its entry? . . . It does not enter through the eyes, for It is not a colour; nor through the ears, for It is not a sound."

Note: Here the experience of the saint and the poet differs. The Word, for a poet, *does* come as a sound. But one from far away.

"Nor by the nostrils, for It does not unite Itself to the air. . . . By what way, then, did It enter? Perhaps It did not enter, for It does not come from without, like an external thing."

Here, again, the experience is different; the material world has delivered up its essence to the visiting angel of the poets.

"Nor does It come from within, since Goodness, I know, is not in me.

"I mounted to the highest part of myself, and higher still reigned the world. Strange exploration, I descended to the depth of myself, and I perceived It in still lower depths. It was more close to me than myself."

But it is a long vigil the saint and the poet endure before that meeting. And it is of the early experience of the poet that I write here—where the poet is merely in touch with the outer world. It is rather like watching the growth of a lily, from root to stem, from stem to flower.

Speaking of my earliest poems, it was suggested by some critics that I was greatly influenced by Diaghileff's Russian Ballet. This was not so, although all artists, in all mediums, were, of course, influenced by it to a certain degree. I was influenced, rather, by the outer surroundings of my childhood. Those influences, however, with the maturing of my childhood, are now far from me.

I was, in the beginning of my work, very strongly influenced by that great composer Stravinsky, although he is an artist in a different medium. A short poem called "Dark Song," for instance, was inspired by a song of his.

> *The fire was furry as a bear*
> *And the flames purr . . .*
> *The brown bear rambles in his chain*
> *Captive to cruel men*
> *Through the dark and hairy wood . . .*
> *The maid sighed, "All my blood*
> *Is animal. They thought I sat*
> *Like a household cat;*
> *But through the dark woods rambled I . . .*
> *Oh, if my blood would die!"*
> *The fire had a bear's fur;*
> *It heard and knew . . .*
> *The dark earth, furry as a bear,*
> *Grumbled too!*

The poem is about the beginning of things and their relationship—the fire, that purrs like an animal and has a beast's thick coat (the crumbling, furry black coal), and a girl whose blood has the dark pulse and instinct of the earth. The long, harsh, animal-purring R's, and the occasional double vowels, as in "bear" and "fire," though these last are divided by a muted R, are intended to convey the uncombatable animal instinct. The poem is built on a scheme of harsh R's, alternating with dulled R's, and the latter, with the thickness of the Br and the Mb in

> *The brown bear rambles in his chain*

are meant to give the thickness of the bear's dull fur. The dissonances of the first line

The fire was furry as a bear

the one-and-a-half syllables of "fire" stretching forward and upward and then breaking, contrasted with the dark, thick, numb insistence of the first syllable in "furry"—the fact that the dissonances ending the first six lines are *dropping* dissonances—this conveys the feeling of the animal's thick paws that have not the power of lifting. The sinking or dulled dissonances which end some of the lines in the place of rhymes— "bear," "purr"—"chain," "men"—the way in which, in the midst of this darkness, there is an occasional high insistent vowel sound—these effects are deliberate and are meant to convey a darkened groping.

In most of these early poems, *Bucolic Comedies*, the experiments are less dealing with rhythm than with sense-transfusion. It was said that the images in these poems were strange. This was partly the result of condensing—partly because, where the language of one sense was insufficient to cover the meaning, the sensation, I used the language of another, and by this means attempted to pierce down to the essence of the thing seen, by discovering it in attributes which at first sight appear alien, but which are acutely related—by producing its quintessential colour (sharper, brighter than that seen by an eye grown stale) and by stripping it of all unessential details.

* * *

The days at Scarborough were like the scales played by a child upon the piano, or raindrops running down the windowpanes.

"Sir George Beaumont," wrote Coleridge, in *Anima Poetae*, "found great advantage through learning to draw from Nature through gauze spectacles."

This, of course, is the mark of the Amateur, who invariably blurs and softens. Nothing could have been less amateur than my brothers and myself. We were born to be professionals. But my father's hope was that I should learn to draw, to see everything, through gauze spectacles. Nothing must have sharp edges, the truth must be comfortably veiled. He wished my brothers and me to be equally semi-adept at everything, and passion for the object seen, or heard, must be rigidly excluded. The less gift we had for anything, the more we were forced to practise it. Games, for instance, we disliked, and were, therefore, made to waste our time on them. Nor were they even supposed to be a recreation, but a means of "keeping up with the Joneses."

Having discovered that I had no talent whatsoever for the pictorial arts, he determined that I should be forced to learn to draw at the local art school, which specialised in a damping-down process of an extraordinary proficiency. Michelangelo and Leonardo could emerge living from this tuition, but I doubt if any lesser painter could have survived it.

The drawing mistress was a kind, woolly, tea-addicted elderly maiden, Miss Alberts, who was always garbed in green serge (this being, I think, a tribute to *Punch's* notion of the pre-Raphaelites). She seemed to have been endowed with a treble ration of shining protuberant teeth, and these were always bared ingratiatingly. She did not *hate* art, she simply ignored it, excepting manually. And her right hand, which seemed to have a life, or rather death, of its own, was completely unconnected with her brain. This disconnected hand of hers guided my still fairly infantile hand to perpetrate a drawing of a plaster cast of a lion, of all subjects. The result may be imagined. Had I been forced to copy a plaster cast of a mouse, the passion of indignation, of injured pride—*my* pride and the fiery pride of the lion—would have been less.

This ineffable drawing still exists and is referred to as Dame Edith's Lion—the lion, I suppose, of the author of "Heart and Mind." *

When I was about twelve years old, my father determined that He (I must really use a capital letter in this connection) must be portrayed for posterity. And the portrait must be a pendant, a Doppelgänger, of the family portrait by Copley that hangs in the dining-room at Renishaw.

After a good deal of fussing, he decided that Sargent was to be the artist whom he would take under his wing, and he set about teaching the gentleman in question his business.

My father was portrayed in riding-dress (he never rode), my mother in a white-spangled low evening gown and a hat with feathers, arranging, with one

* See the poem, pages 49–50.

prettily shaped, flaccid, entirely useless hand, red anemones in a silver bowl (she never arranged flowers, and in any case it would have been a curious occupation for one wearing a ball-dress, even if, at the same time, she wore a hat).

The colour of the anemones was repeated in my scarlet dress. I was white with fury and contempt, and indignant that my father held me in what he thought was a tender paternal embrace. (I was freed from my Bastille during the period of the sittings.) Osbert and Sacheverell, sitting on the floor, playing with my mother's black pug, were the only beings that seemed to have any trace of life. Mr. Sargent, a kind and charming man, kept them more or less quiet by reciting to them the following verse, repeated at intervals:

> *There was a young lady of Spain*
> *Who always was sick in the train—*
> *Not once and again,*
> *Or again and again—*
> *But again and again and again.*

The portrait was painted against the background of one of the great Renishaw tapestries—depicting Justice, as it happened.

HEART AND MIND

Said the Lion to the Lioness—"When you are amber
  dust—
No more a raging fire like the heat of the Sun
(No liking but all lust) —

49

Remember still the flowering of the amber blood and
  bone,
The rippling of bright muscles like a sea,
Remember the rose-prickles of bright paws,
Though we shall mate no more
Till the fire of that sun the heart and the moon-cold
  bone are one."

Said the Skeleton lying upon the sands of Time—
"The great gold planet that is the mourning heat of the
  sun
Is greater than all gold, more powerful
Than the tawny body of a Lion that fire consumes
Like all that grows or leaps . . . so is the heart
More powerful than all dust. Once I was Hercules
Or Samson, strong as the pillars of the seas:
But the flames of the heart consumed me, and the mind
Is but a foolish wind."

Said the Sun to the Moon—"When you are but a lonely
  white crone,
And I, a dead King in my golden armour somewhere
  in a dark wood,
Remember only this of our hopeless love:
That never till Time is done
Will the fire of the heart and the fire of the mind be
  one."

50

CHAPTER FOUR

The Boarding-House

In the same spring that had seen the Sargent portrait finished, my adenoids had to be removed, and on the advice of Mr. Stout, I, my Bastille, and Miss King-Church, Osbert's and my governess, left Scarborough once again for London, where we stayed at a boarding-house near Lancaster Gate.

The road in which the boarding-house stood was lined on both sides by flowering fruit-trees, bringing a cruel memory of youth to the inhabitants of the house, beings who, with the exception of the one male who passed his life there, looked so immeasurably old that it seemed as if, like the Piltdown Skull, they could not really be as old as their appearance suggested.

The superannuated spinsters who had come to spend their last years in the boarding-house—and, if you come to think of it, there would not be much change from their life to their death—must have been, I think, in their earlier days governesses to rich children. These they seemed to hold in affection, and once in every three years or so their pupils, now grown-up, would come to see them, bringing little presents and reducing their former instructresses to tears of happiness.

Otherwise, nothing ever happened to them, although they were roused at every mealtime to animation and approbation by the diatribes against the proletariat, politicians, youth, and the world in general, by Dicky Wilkins, a gentleman with a small income. He was the only male boarder and gave them, as the late Herr Hitler gave his listeners, the feeling of Joy through Strength. He disapproved, particularly, of feebleness.

He was greatly prized by the old ladies, who saw in him, middle-aged as he was, the hope of the New Generation who would urge on the nations of the world to war and complete annihilation (although, of course, Dicky and they themselves would be left, unmolested, to a cosy world of little intimate tea parties).

Dicky was not tall, and he had a figure which he himself would have been the first to describe as slight. But it was not thin: it seemed, indeed, though there were no protuberances at any point, as if it was ever so slightly padded—as if a thin layer of cotton wool had been placed between Dicky and his clothes, in order to protect him, not only from the cold weather, but from the world. When he walked, it seemed as if all his movements, from the waist downwards, were checked and restrained by a gentlemanly and discreet boa-constrictor. His face, with its heavy flapping eyelids, his half-open, feebly flopping mouth (yes, alas, although feebleness was his bugbear), gave him, in conjunction with his gently rounded figure, a striking resemblance

52

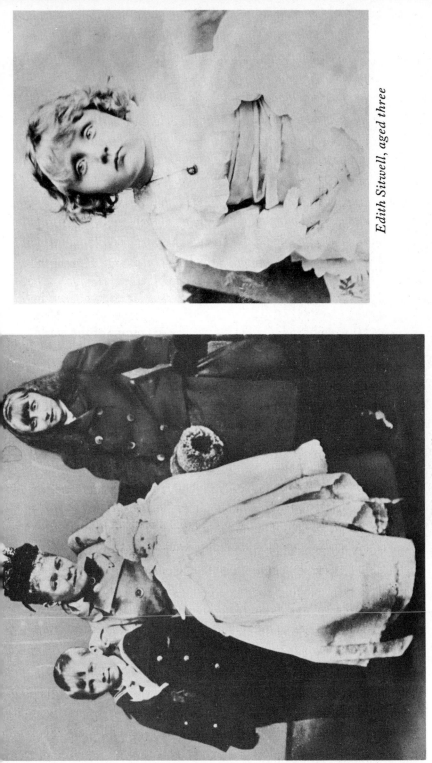

Edith Sitwell, aged three

Osbert, Sacheverell, and Edith Sitwell
with their nurse, Davis, in 1898

The Sitwell Family *by J. S. Sargent, 1900*

Edith Sitwell in eighteenth-century costume

Edith Sitwell in the garden at Renishaw

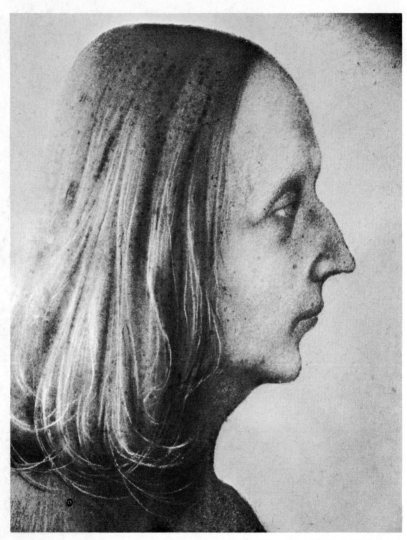

A recently found portrait of Edith Sitwell by Pavel Tchelitchew

The drawing given to Edith Sitwell by Walter Sickert
Wyndham Lewis' portrait of Edith Sitwell

"Plantagenet features and deep-set eyes"
—thus Edith Sitwell described her own appearance

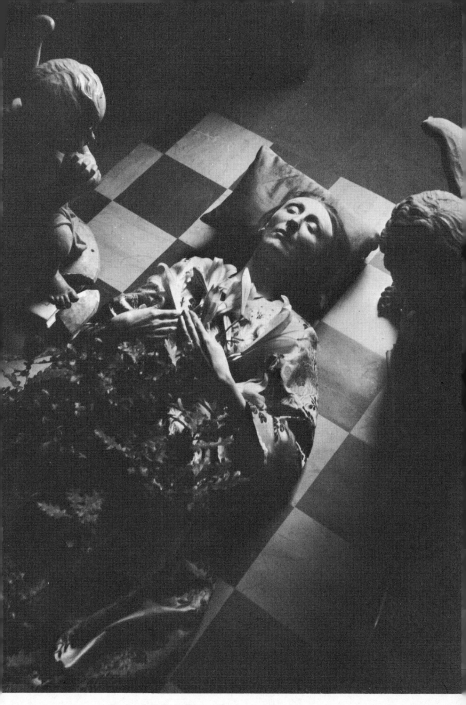

*One of Edith Sitwell's favourites among
the many Cecil Beaton photographs of her*

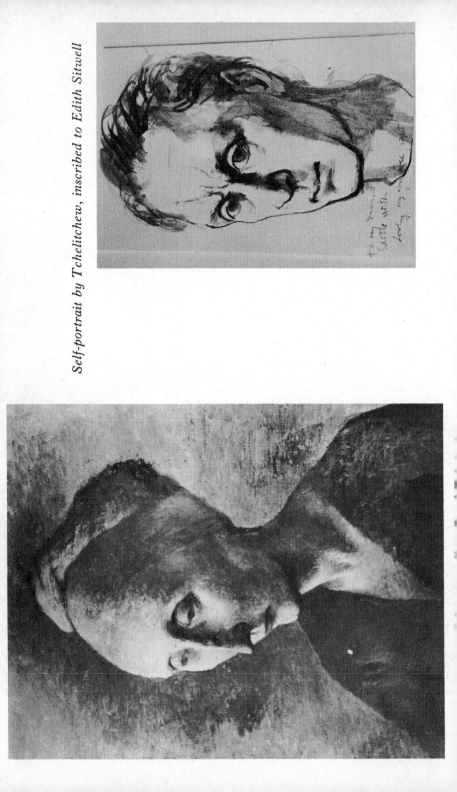

Self-portrait by Tchelitchew, inscribed to Edith Sitwell

The most famous of Tchelitchew's six portraits of Edith Sitwell

A formidable literary trio—Edith, Sacheverell, and Osbert Sitwell

*Edith Sitwell wearing one of the rings that started
arguments among her audiences in America*

*A party at the Gotham Book Mart, New York, in 1948, honouring
Edith and Osbert Sitwell (seated, center). In the left foreground,
William Rose Benét; behind him, Stephen Spender; behind him,
Horace Gregory and his wife, Marya Zaturenska. At the back (left
to right), Tennessee Williams, Richard Eberhart, Gore Vidal, José
García Villa, and W. H. Auden (on ladder). At right, Elizabeth
Bishop (standing), Marianne Moore, Randall Jarrell, and Delmore
Schwartz (foreground). On the floor, center, Charles Henri Ford.*

Edith Sitwell during an American visit, in 1948
(*the hand holding the cigar is Osbert Sitwell's*)

Edith Sitwell listening to a playback of one of her recordings, 1953

Edith Sitwell with Aldous and Maria Huxley in California, 1953

*Edith Sitwell at a rehearsal for a concert at the Royal
Festival Hall, London, held in celebration of her seventy-
fifth birthday, with (left to right) Sacheverell Sitwell,
Sir William Walton, Sacheverell Sitwell's son, and Osbert Sitwell.*

to an unfledged bird that had fallen out of its nest.

At moments, when talking to the admiring circle of old ladies, he would adopt, perhaps for protection, a light, frivolous manner (for he prided himself on this frivolousness, masking a deep nature, a wisdom and foresight as striking as his wit). On these occasions he seemed, when speaking, to be nibbling chickweed. But in those moments when the god spoke through his mouth, when he, modest as he was (and he was very modest), became the Oracle, the mouthpiece of the judgment against which there could be no appeal, his mouth would open and shut until he presented much the appearance of a newly hatched chicken suffering from the pip. On these occasions his modesty was even more striking than usual. Taking off his pince-nez, he would polish them, casting down his eyes meanwhile, and flapping his eyelids rapidly, whilst through his mouth would sound the Oracle, denouncing the government, the times, the feebleness of the age. Sometimes the Oracle, in its wish to reform, to stem the descent of the age before its final downfall, would utter the awful threat that if all was not changed, if the voice of the Oracle (alias Dicky) crying in the wilderness was not heeded, he, Dicky, would "turn his back on Civilisation."

Madame Baker, the mistress of the boarding-house, one scarcely saw by daylight, at least as a suffering human creature. She had swaddled her whole being, in order to protect herself against the cruel mockery that pursues the defenceless, the poverty, the hopelessness of those whose only crumbling defence against the world was the façade of youth (laughter masquerading as sympathy). She had so wrapped herself in the memories of imaginary scenes and triumphs, to protect herself from the reality of her poverty, her hopeless outlook, that she now no longer remembered her life as it had been in truth.

The boarding-house and its mistress always seemed to be reigned over by a bustling joyless day. But at night all superficialities were necessarily laid aside, as the inhabitants of that house undressed before entering the sleep which was but the forerunner of a sleep longer and more dreamless.

I remember one such spring night when all living creatures were stripped down to their essentials.

Outside the house, the storm of young petals, glittering and wind-thin, seemed wet as if with tears, some warm and flushed with youth, some flying as if they were being pursued by the young and ardent wind of spring; these, with the hailstorm of sharp white buds, blown by that wind, pelted the windows with a faint dying sound, melted like snow on the dark paths. It seemed as if the whole world was filled with these corollas, flushed with the cold, trembling as their petals shrank together at the touch of the young wind.

Upstairs, in her bedroom, Madame Baker was preparing for bed.

One felt that when she took off her dress at night the act was like the undamming of Noah's Flood.

This enormous woman, with her thick and muffled face and neck, when she was fully painted and equipped for the sad and hopeless business of the day, looked, when static, like an effigy of one of the Deadly Sins (swollen by some meaningless importance), the figurehead of Greed or Envy, carried at the head of some purposeless procession. Her vast size gave her an unwieldy, lumbering gait, a shambling walk, so that she seemed always to be in at least four places at once; and this, added to the fact that her animation was such that she appeared to be, not one being, but an increasing multitude, gave those confronted with her the feeling that it was impossible to escape from her, that they must, inevitably, be run over.

So, bobbling and plunging as if she was a long line of sea-elephants facing the surge of waves, she faced the poverty of her days.

Her eyes, when fully mascaraed, were deliberately roguish, but had, at the same time, a look of hard and deliberate greed which was borne out by the whole contour of her face. But now, alone in her room, the paint washed away from eyes, cheeks, and lips, her poor fat flabby cheeks were pathetic; they drooped in a sad and dispirited way. Her eyes were no longer greedy: they were the eyes of a very old child. They were even kind, and the sadness—because she had been robbed by cruel elders (cruel youth, so much older, harder, more cynical than herself) of something for which she had hoped—contained nothing of bitterness. You would never have known this old and bewildered child for the same being who, protected from the world by a glistening coat of paint and of pretence, confronted poverty, the cruel eye of day, the small mouse-fretting worries of each hour, with such gallantry.

Indeed, her being by night and her being by day might not have sprung from the same original stem. By day, she held her head in such a position that she might have been tossing it when the wind changed and, in so doing, transfixed her. When she greeted acquaintances of whom she did not approve and whom she wished to impress, she held her right hand above her head—rather in the manner of one who is training a dog to beg for sugar. She was much addicted to stateliness, and often confessed that she could imagine herself "standing at the top of a marble staircase—*receiving*," although the identity of the persons to be received was left in doubt. "You ought to have been an ambassadress, dear," her friends would say, admiringly.

Nobody knew, with any certainty, what had been Madame Baker's origin, or who her husband had been. If questioned about the latter, she would say, vaguely, "Somebody very important, dear . . . in Vienna. But I am not allowed to say *what!*" And she would remain silent for a moment, seeing, in her mind's eye, the original of the photograph hidden in a drawer upstairs, the glistening being with the spreading waistcoat, and that moist fly-trap for little insignificant fly-by-nights, the luxuriant tropical vegetation springing from his upper lip.

Poor Bert. It was those women! Ah well!

About matters other than her husband she was more communicative and liked to spread an air of Continental broadmindedness round herself, talking much of "the old days in Vienna," where, as she let slip from time to time, she had been the acknowledged toast and beauty.

Now, in the spring night, something of its poignance and beauty brought to her memories of those imagined days and nights. Ah dear! What a time that had been! The gaiety! Never in bed before three o'clock! The champagne! The glitter! Ah well, one was young then!

But there were moments now when she could not remember if it was really true that each night, when she entered a restaurant with her train of cavaliers, the whole assemblage rose and toasted her—she could not remember if it was really true that the Grand Dukes had drunk champagne out of her slippers. Had it happened to her? Or had she read about it somewhere? It *must* have happened to her, surely? She had told the story so often.

And now what was left to her? Only small snatched-at comforts. And, turning out the light and wallowing in her bed, she determined that next morning she would pretend to be asleep when she heard Annie pass the door, so that she would not be obliged to get up and make the early-morning tea. Yes, she would pretend to be asleep, so that Annie would have to bring her a cup of tea in order to wake her.

Upstairs, in her small room, standing before the strip of stained and dulled looking-glass, Annie by day and Greta by night, with her hair released from the restrictions imposed by "that damned old cat," was curving her neck and blinking her eyes at the image she saw reflected in the glass; she looked admiringly and lovingly at the glamorous creature who lay hidden so mysteriously behind the pale face with the long nose and the light eyes, the undergrown body with its youthful flat bosom.

Raising her arms, her work-worn hands, above her head, she contemplated that glamorous figure in the glass.

Tick-tock-tick-tock. Time was passing. The sound of its creaking tread was louder than that of the young flower petals upon the windowpanes. Annie by day and Greta by night looked at the cheap clock upon her mantelpiece. Half past eleven—half past eleven! The glamorous creature who came to visit her each night must soon leave her, for at six o'clock next morning the clock on the mantelpiece would summon its slave.

She thought of Bob, the gardener's boy at Mon Tresor, down the road. He had given her a sprig of almond blossom yesterday. Silly, wasn't it?

Now all the lights in the house were extinguished. Dicky Wilkins, lying on his side, his mouth open, one arm flung across his face, had fulfilled the dire threat made by the Oracle—that threat for which the world had been waiting. He had turned his back on Civilisation (and serve it right! It had been warned often enough!). Fearless and alone, he had gone to that wild world which was in tune with his own nature. What was there to fear for such a man?

Yet what was that distant, that blood-chilling sound —that ever nearing, crashing, tearing, roaring tempest of sound? An elephant, uprooting the vastest trees in the jungle, throwing the vegetable monsters into the primeval mud, trampling on them with its giant feet, trumpeting in its mad triumph!

Dicky sat up in bed, sweating and shivering.

The mouse, with a final squeal, bit through the wainscoting and scampered across the room into its mouse-hole.

CHAPTER FIVE

The Primulas Had Meant No Harm

As a child and a very young girl, I spent a good deal of time with my two grandmothers, with my maternal grandmother at Londesborough and with Lady Sitwell in her small country house (Hay-Brow, near Scarborough), surrounded by flowers, like buzzing summer lights, or a sweet Mozartean tune. These were tended by her Belgian gardener, Ernest de Taeye, who would have been like a dear great lumbering bear had he not been completely bald, the result of touching a certain kind of primula. He spoke of flowers tenderly, as fathers sometimes (I suppose) speak of their children, and he touched them with an equal tenderness—the primulas had meant no harm.

He wore, as always, because of his baldness, a straw hat which had some of the appearance of a bee-hive. He bore a strong resemblance to a Flemish portrait.

Osbert has produced, in a poem, a lovely and loving portrait of Mrs. de Taeye.

I remember my grandmother Sitwell's household more clearly when she had removed to Gosden, her house in Surrey. Here again, one was surrounded by a world of flowers.

Thinking of that world now, I am reminded of this lovely passage from the sainted, illuminated madman Christopher Smart, in "Rejoice with the Lamb":

For there is no Height on which there are not flowers.
For flowers have great virtues for all the senses.
For the flower glorifies God and the root parries the
  adversary.
For the flowers have their angels even the words of
  God's Creation.
For the warp and the woof of flowers are worked by
  perpetual moving spirits.
For elegant phrases are nothing but flowers.
For flowers are peculiarly the poetry of Christ.
For the right names of flowers are yet in heaven.
God makes gardeners better nomenclators.

With the exception of Frank, the butler (who seemed, though not young, still younger than some of the others), and an under-housemaid and a kitchen maid, pink as Ernest's primulas, and whose giggles had been frozen into muteness, my grandmother Sitwell's servants were so ancient that they seemed to have strayed out of the eighteenth century.

Frank had a grave, dog-like, darkish face with a pointed nose. He and Musk, one of my grandmother's

Samoyed dogs, appeared to have taken on each other's personality, and, as far as *faces* were concerned, each other's face.

Frank was discretion itself. One never knew what was going on in his mind. He never spoke, in our presence, excepting to announce meals, or that the carriage was at the door. He had great tact, as, for instance, when on one occasion, at family prayers, I, then seventeen years old, disgraced myself. It was my turn to choose and read aloud a chapter from the Bible, and I started to read a passage from the Song of Solomon. Unfortunately, I was so overcome by the innocent demeanour of my Aunt Florence, and the reverent attitude of the parrot, who had the habit of covering his face with one claw when the household was assembled to join together in prayer, that I fell into paroxysms of laughter. Frank, with an immovable face, rose, shepherded his flock from the room, then, when the noise of my hysteria had ceased, returned with them as if nothing had happened.

My grandmother's incredibly ancient lady's maid, Leckly, had been with her, when I knew her, for sixty years. She was the original of Mrs. Troy in my long poem (which is largely about my life as a child and young girl) "The Sleeping Beauty." The mise en scène, however, was Londesborough. The whole atmosphere of the poem is that which I knew at Londesborough when I was a child and a young girl. (Malinn was one of the Londesborough housemaids. So was "the gossiping naiad of the water," and the other country maids, with their butter-yellow satin hair.)

Then, underneath the dancing, glancing bough
Came Malinn, with her round cheeks dyed as pink
As the insipid empty-tasting fruits
Of summer giggling through the rounded leaves.

Outside the stillroom was a cherry tree,
And through the dancing shadows she could see
Cross ancient Poll Troy come to do her duty. . . .
She had a cold frost-bitten beauty
Like blue moonlight smooth and cold
As amber; with her trembling old
Hands she tied the boughs aloft
Through the air all creamy soft;
Then on the sill of the woodland dairy,
Moving as quick and light as a fairy,
She put a bowl of the thickest cream
(As thick as chestnut flowers in a dream).
The gossiping naiad of the water,
In her sprigged gown like the housekeeper's
  daughter,
Giggles outside the stillroom; she
Plucks at the thick-bustled cherry tree.
And Poll is cross; she chases cherried
Country maids like thickest-berried
Cherry trees in their ruched gown
Till they run from the palace, down,
Like the sprigged muslin waterfalls
Of this clear country, to where calls
Pan, with his satyrs on the rocks
Feeding their wave-weary flocks.

The naiad's giggling irritates
Cross Poll Troy till at last she rates
Her through the thick-leaved cherry tree:
"My eyes are dim—I yet can see
You, lazy queen! Go work!" "I can't."
"I say you shall!" "I say I shan't!"
"But when the airs are creamy soft
And candle-flames are quince flowers, oft
Though my heart flutters like a bird,
All dream-dark, though as soft as curd
The moonlight seems still, from my bed
I rise and work, you sleepyhead!
Though I am dim and very old,
I wake the flames all jewel-cold,
The flames that seem, when they soar high,
Like waterfalls of jewels; you sigh,
While I, Miss, churn and make the curd,"
Piped Poll Troy like a small cross bird,
Then shuts the stillroom window, goes, for she
Still hears the naiad giggling through the tree.

Leckly, although she was my grandmother Sitwell's
lady's maid—and nothing could have been more dis-
similar than my two grandmothers' households—
seemed a more suitable inmate of Londesborough Park
than of Hay-Brow and Gosden. The eighteenth-century
luxury of Londesborough was remarkable in its opu-
lence. Hay-Brow and Gosden were reigned over by
comfort rather than luxury. For my grandmother
Londesborough was one of the great hostesses of the
age, whereas my grandmother Sitwell and my Aunt

Florence could be best described as Lambeth Palace Lounge-Lizards, since, as Archbishop Tait was my father's great-uncle and guardian, his mother and sister spent much of their time in that fortress of mouldering peace and moribund history, and both ladies smelt faintly of long-used prayer-books and the red cloth of hassocks. At Lambeth my aunt met "a musical little Mr. Maxwell" and a Mr. Somebody-or-Other who told, at dinner, "a most *horrid* story about the Millennium." But neither of those gentlemen would, I think, have been appreciated at Londesborough.

Both my grandmothers suffered from troubles of a hirsute nature. My grandmother Sitwell's was fraught with more danger, as it was impossible to guess where her hair would be found next. After my grandmother had taken a house in London, sometimes these two coils (one destined for the top of her head, the other for the back) would take refuge in Leckly's back pocket, and she, forgetting this, would go shopping in Oxford Street and Regent Street, whereupon her two charges would attempt to escape from their temporary home, arousing in the spectators (from the very nature and place from which they emerged) the conjecture that Leckly was an escapee from the Zoological Gardens.

Deprived of her crowning glories, my grandmother would be obliged to take to her bed until Leckly could remember where those adornments had been put—for she feared the all-seeing eyes of her regiment of curates. I am *not* denigrating the ministers of the Low Church —earnest, self-sacrificing, infinitely helpful to their flocks, and sadly underpaid—but my grandmother adopted unfortunate examples such as are found in every Church. These examples were at once particularly smooth and particularly uncultured. They had, so to speak, a spiritual smell as of a winter garden full of mouldering cabbages, and were, for the most part, exactly of that colour.

Long, lank black hair descended on to the backs of their collars, which seemed to have taken on the hue and texture of these. It was rare for them to smoke—even cigarettes. But if they did so, they bore the expression of one faced by a particularly ferocious and treacherous lion.

My grandmother had an especial pet—an imitation curate who differed but slightly from the real ones. He infested her house from the time when I was about fifteen years old.

He bore a distinct resemblance to a bat, although he did not hang head downwards, but was horribly upright, physically as well as mentally. He was about twenty-three years of age, and a born battener.

He wore a signet ring, patent-leather pumps at breakfast, and he carried a handkerchief in his sleeve. To my mother, all three of these phenomena seemed worse than the First Fall of Man.

My grandmother lingered lovingly over his Christian name, which she pronounced Haa'wwy!

Years after the time of which I write, Haa'wwy produced an autobiography—for what reason I have been unable to discover, as nobody, with the exception of the genuine curates, my grandmother, my infuriated mother, and her offspring, had ever heard of him. In this work, he told the reader that an admirer had described him as "a Very Quiet Gentleman."

He may have been *quiet*, but he was *not* a *gentleman*.

My grandmother Londesborough's hirsute troubles were less poignant than those of Lady Sitwell, as everybody was terrified of her and nobody dared to giggle in her presence.

Lady Londesborough's footmen (who constituted as large a regiment as that of my grandmother Sitwell's curates) were forbidden to look at each other in her presence, or to speak excepting in their professional capacity. They might speak to Martin, the butler, but on no account were they to look at him. Otherwise, their silence was only broken at their extreme peril.

My grandmother Londesborough never spoke to any of the servants excepting the butler, Martin, and the old housekeeper, Mrs. Selby, who had a face like a large red strawberry, covered with faint silvery hair. She is the original of one of the protagonists in my poem "Three Poor Witches":

> *When she walks,*
> *Turned to a wreath*
> *Is every hedge;*
> *She walks beneath*
> *Flowered trees like water*
> *Splashing down;*
> *Her rich and dark silk*
> *Plumcake gown*
> *Has folds so stiff*
> *It stands alone*

Within the fields
When she is gone.

One evening at the beginning of November, my
grandmother (who was then at Londesborough Lodge
in Scarborough) went up to bed with her hair of the
usual brown colour. Next morning, when she came
down, at eleven o'clock, to an enormous breakfast (eggs
and bacon, cold grouse, ham, cold partridge, home-
made buns and buttercup-coloured cream and butter,
hothouse peaches and grapes), the autumnal hue of her
hair had changed to the most snow-bound of winters.
My aunts, not daring to appear conscious of this phenomenon, stared at their plates. My grandfather concentrated on the breast of a cold partridge. The footmen
seemed to be bound, more than ever, in a spell of
silence.

My grandmother's white wig—for such it was—appeared at the most opportune moment, for the date was
the 5th of November, a day (I may remind my American readers) dedicated to the memory of Guy Fawkes,
who had plotted to blow up the Houses of Parliament,
and was then celebrated by children wheeling a peram-
bulator containing a battered-looking dummy and begging for "a penny for the poor guy."

After breakfast, on this auspicious occasion, my
grandmother took up her usual place in a bath-chair at
the entrance of the Londesborough Lodge gardens.

Seated against a background of a frieze of captive
daughters and a melancholy-looking footman, she must
have presented a remarkable appearance. So much so
that a very small curate, who was accompanied by his

wife and multitudinous children, seeing her and remembering the date and its implications, placed a penny in her lap, saying, genially, "Remember, remember, the fifth of November." Then, with his wife and children, he entered the gardens, which were private.

The gift was *not* well received. At first my grandmother was deprived of speech. At last, recovering it, she said over her shoulder to the footman, "Tell Martin to come to me!"

When that dignitary appeared, my grandmother told him of the outrage to which she had been subjected, and ordered him to gather together all the footmen and gardeners, and to chase the culprit and his family out of the grounds.

Whether they were caught or not, history does not relate. My grandmother never referred to the subject again. But the silence enjoined on the footmen must have been difficult to sustain, once they were out of her presence.

If the curate *was* captured and expelled, he must have presented the appearance of Dionysus after the Maenads had finished with him. His pursuers would never have dared allow him to escape in one piece.

My grandmother Sitwell's favourite virtue was, perhaps, that known as charity. But hers was of a peculiar kind.

She had never *really* succeeded in *liking* St. Mary Magdalen, who had, to be frank, a rather horrid Roman Catholic air about her. And yet she felt bound to accept her, in a cold manner, owing to the passages in the New Testament. It was, perhaps, owing to this forced acceptance on my grandmother's part that she determined to wrap equally deplorable young persons in an unescapable charity.

Therefore she and a Suffragan Bishop, with a frostbitten appearance like something on a cheap Christmas card, would, on hot summer evenings at Scarborough, make sorties together in her barouche, driven by her old coachman, Hill. Encircling the town, they would surround and capture any young woman who appeared to them to be unsuitably dressed and in a deplorable "state of joyosity," as John Knox called it.

Aided by Hill, my grandmother and the Bishop would seize these unfortunates and decant them into a red brick house known as The Home, where, supervised by Sister Edith, the matron, a bursting woman like an advertisement for tomatoes in a railway station, they earned their living by tearing our laundry to shreds every week.

It was one of the rules of The Home that every kidnapped young person must, immediately on her arrival, be given a bath under the supervision of Sister Edith. They were then encased in twill nightgowns, like strait waistcoats. Next morning they were forced to put on the Home uniform, hideous navy-blue coats and skirts, and boots like those worn by policemen in years past. With this attire they wore shapeless navy-blue felt hats. Sister Edith seemed to be bursting out of a parody of a nun's habit; she ascribed this phenomenon to the fact that she was a Deaconess (whatever that may be).

Four times a year the captives were commanded to

70

"enjoy themselves." This entailed bursting into song, accompanied on a harmonium by Sister Edith. The performance started with a solemn rendering of "The Lost Chord," followed by a singularly horrible setting of John Greenleaf Whittier's "The Barefoot Boy."

> *Blessings on thee, little man,*
> *Barefoot boy, with cheek of tan!*
> *With thy turned-up pantaloons,*
> *And thy merry whistled tunes.*

(Oh, *certainly* bless him! I am all for it!)

My grandmother and my Aunt Florence entered thoroughly into the "joyosity." And the regiment of curates were hoarded like a treasure at the end of the room, and sternly forbidden to look at the captives.

As we have seen, each fresh captive was bathed, immediately on arrival, under the auspices of Sister Edith. But one evening a slim, particularly youthful-looking captive was decanted into The Home. In spite of Sister Edith's threats of physical violence, this new arrival defied her and refused to give any reason for this defiance, remaining unbathed. Some time later it was discovered that every single inmate of The Home was about to give birth. My grandmother, smoothing down her gloves, said that this phenomenon was, no doubt, due to the Transit of Venus. But Sister Edith, in the presence of my grandmother, caught and succeeded in disrobing this latest arrival at The Home.

It was then discovered that the Transit of Venus was in no way involved in the mystery of the forthcoming fruitfulness among the captives. It was due to the be-

haviour of a flippant young man who had taken a dislike
to the Bishop, and who, dressed as a girl, had seized on
this method for discomforting him.

I do not remember for what reason The Home was
disbanded. I know only that after my grandmother's
death my Aunt Florence was "taken care of" by Sister
Edith, who helped herself to everything within reach.
She was much prized by my father because of her
constant mischief-making. At last Osbert, then sta-
tioned at Chelsea Barracks, became tired of this, and he
and a young friend of his, having told my mother that
she would receive this letter, wrote to her as follows:

My Lady,
It breaks my heart, yes, and the hearts of *all* the
tenants, to see you and your three dear children
living in want whilst Sir George squanders money
on the Scarlet Woman.

(Sister Edith had, for some time, seemed in imminent
danger of bursting and was redder than ever.)

When a fortnight had elapsed during which my
mother resolutely refused to speak to my father, she at
last showed him the letter. He flew into a passion and,
rushing upstairs into Mr. Hollingworth's office,* told
him he intended to place the letter in the hands of the
local police.

Mr. Hollingworth remained calm, but asked if he
might see the letter.

"Certainly, Mr. Hollingworth."

"I wouldn't take this too seriously if I were you, Sir

*Mr. Hollingworth is our friend, and the agent of the estate.

George. It is only Captain Osbert at it again."

Whereupon my father wrote a furious letter to his errant son: "To accuse *anyone*, let alone a parent, of adultery is a crime punishable by life imprisonment."

Osbert wrote to him, in answer to this:

> My dearest Father, my young friend and I are horrified to realise the crime we have, unwittingly, committed! We *had* heard of adultery, but when we asked the Chaplain to explain to us the meaning of this, he told us it meant "being grown up."

My father was delighted with this letter, and the proof that, in spite of having gone through the 1914–1918 war, Osbert had retained his youthful innocence.

CHAPTER SIX

Long Ago, Many Years Ago

Long ago, many years ago . . . I remember staying with my grandmother Sitwell at Bath, where she had taken a house.

The delicate leafless cold seemed about to bud into those flowers, the first young flakes of snow. Old ladies in bath-chairs were being whirled round and round the Roman moon-coloured crescents, were being whirled round and round by bath-chairmen who behaved as if they were typhoons; while, behind them, their captive women tugged at the old ladies' bath-chairs as if the old ladies were kites and might at any moment fly over the houses, away and away.

Outside a stuffy bookshop, two maiden ladies were on the pavement lost in speculation. The elder of these wore a long dress which burst into a thousand leaves and waterfalls and branches and minor worries. She had hair of the costliest gold thread, bright as the gold in a

74

fourteenth-century missal, and this, when undone, fell in a waterfall till it nearly reached her feet. But at this moment it was crammed beneath a hat which seemed to have been decorated with all the exports of our colonies —ostrich feathers, fruits, furs, and heaven knows what besides. Her eyes were blue as a saint's eyes, and were mild as a spring wind.

The younger maiden lady, then aged about eighteen, had the remote elegance and distinction of a very tall bird. Indeed, her gown had the feathery quality of a bird's raiment, and one would not have been surprised, at any moment, if she had preened her quills. She stood there, in the delicate leafless cold, with her long thin legs poised upon the wet pavement as some great bird stands in a pool. She had not the look of one who has many acquaintances—not more, perhaps, than a few leafless flowering boughs and blackthorn boughs, and the early and remote flakes of the snow. Her only neighbour was the silence, and her voice had more the sound of a woodwind instrument than of a human voice. She was plain and knew it. "An eighteenth-century memoir, Edith," the older lady was saying, "is what your Grannie would like—giving the life of the times."

"Give me, if you please," she said shyly, as she entered the shop, "some eighteenth-century memoirs," and retired with the works of Casanova. Memoirs indeed, but the life of the times, eventually, failed to please the eldest lady, for whom the life was intended. "And *I* should like, if you please," said the youngest lady, "some poems of Swinburne. . . . Have you . . . ?" "Oh no, Miss," said the shopman, flustered and shocked, "we have nothing of that kind. But should you care for the works of Laurence Hope, which are also full of love interest . . . " The youngest lady did not think she would care for these, and, aunt and niece, they floated out again.

"It is not too cold," said Miss Florence Sitwell, hopefully, "for a little drive." And stepping into an unusually sprightly-looking if ghostly victoria, they went for a little drive in the dream-country.

These places were among the green landscapes of my very early youth, landscapes scattered with "des plantations prodigieuses où les gentilshommes sauvages chassent leurs chroniques sous la lumière qu'on a créé."

In these countrysides, the people know that Destiny is reported, and has feathers like a hen. There I have seen pig-snouted darkness grunting and rooting in the hovels. The very clouds are like crazy creaking wooden chalets filled with emptiness, and the leaves have an animal fleshiness. And here, beneath the hairy and bestial skies of winter, the country gentlemen are rooted in the mould; and they know that beyond the hairy and bestial aspects of the sky (that harsh and goatish tent) something hides: but they have forgotten what it is. So they wander, aiming with their guns at mocking feathered creatures that have learned the wonder and secret of movement, beneath clouds that are so low-hung that they seem nothing but wooden potting-sheds for the no-longing disastrous stars (they will win the prize at the local flower-show). The waters of the shallow lake gurgle like a stoat, murderously; the little unfledged feathers of the foam have forgotten how to fly, and the country gentlemen wander, hunting for something, hunting.

Now it was time to return to the house in the moon-coloured crescent.

CHAPTER SEVEN

The Sound of Marching Footsteps

Now, on rainy nights, I am haunted by the sound of marching footsteps.

Only the rain? Or ceaseless tears, as the six million ghosts of youth rise from the grave of the world—the town called Sarajevo.

I intend to write but little of the 1914–1918 war. The history of this should be left to the men who remained after enduring the whole physical horrors brought upon them by this universal madness.

In the night of the 3rd–4th August, 1914, the whole of the human race became one family, with the same family history of suffering and fear, with the terrible goodbyes to sons, brothers, husbands. (I shall be haunted always by the agonising cry in one letter from a young soldier at the Front read by Osbert in his duty as censor: "Don't forget me. . . . Don't forget me. . . . Don't forget me!")

78

Osbert left Renishaw to rejoin his regiment, the Grenadier Guards, in the middle of the night before war broke out. He was convalescing after a serious illness. For this reason he had to undergo a month's training before he could be sent to the Front. I must always be grateful to that illness, for all his young friends, with the exception of two, were killed in the first month of the war.

I have lived through the shattering of two civilisations, have seen two Pandora's boxes opened. One contained horror, the other emptiness.

"The fifth element is mud," said Napoleon.

In both the new worlds hatched in those Pandora's boxes, mud and flies had taken over the spirit. (Pascal exclaimed in *Les Pensées:* "The Power of flies! They win battles, hinder our soul from acting, eat our body!")

Merle Armitage, in his foreword to Louis Danz's *Dynamic Dissonance*, quoted Danz as saying, "Oh, if Lazarus had only written a book!" He added, "Eugene O'Neill broods and dreams, and then wrote Lazarus laughed."

Perhaps the 1914–1918 war was the book written by Lazarus. But nobody laughed.

In the late Louis-Ferdinand Céline's great book *Voyage au Bout de la Nuit*, a doctor in a lunatic asylum, infected by the lunacy around him, utters this appalling phrase: "Nothing exists, Monsieur Baryton, between the penis and mathematics. Nothing at all. It's a vacuum."

To what has the world with all its inhabitants been reduced by the 1914 war and that which came later?

In another of the greatest books written in our time, Sacheverell's *Splendours and Miseries*, occurs this passage, describing an old madwoman in her small madhouse room, "watching a peepshow of demonology, as large as life, taking place within the room. . . . Her visions had, of course, degenerated, and become richer by that degradation and, always, she was the one person who was untouched by them. Whatever happened, she was always safe. That was one manner in which her mania affected her. Therefore, it had become something of a pleasurable sensation. She never smiled but certainly was satisfied and complacent. . . . She is a poor old madwoman. . . . Her malady is not religious mania. It is not so reasonable. It is the melting or liquidation of all images and the disintegration of the world, and everything in it goes to destruction. She is the chosen witness and no harm will come to her. It is the placid wickedness of those who watch and do not try to interfere. . . . She is sitting in judgment, to the extent that all is done with her approval, and her perpetual compliance, did she but know it, is proof that all the visions come from within."

(As, did we but know it, the appalling visions that we now see were born from our inner madness.) This portrait of an old madwoman might be the epitome of our present civilisation.

In the same book, the writer speaks of the approaching anti-Christ for whom the world is ready. "He may be born already, in a flat, or in a summer bungalow where the asphalt ends in nothing, and the new houses are not yet built. In a caravan or trailer. Under a piece of sackcloth propped on sticks; or in the town of petrol tins. . . .

"The beggar king marching out of the slums, or up out of the mines. He and his men have everything to gain and nothing to lose, meaning that in the end they will lose everything and gain nothing. . . .

"Are there no colours in this world of ours?

"There are none, none, none. Only the love, or bravery of the common man."

Some months after the outbreak of war, the sordid tragedy in which my mother was involved, and of which I cannot write at length because it would be too painful both for my brothers and my readers, burst into full flower. This tragedy, which seemed a dwarfish imitation of the universe of mud and flies, affected more my brothers and myself (and especially Osbert, who was the completely innocent victim of her fear, the wish to save her own skin) than my mother and father. My mother, as I have said, knew fear, otherwise she and my father knew nothing, felt nothing excepting their wish to escape from the results of that which she had, out of sheer stupidity, done. Their lives were completely atrophied. All *she* wanted was to return to her silly daily life of bridge and watching the golfers on the golf-course. All he wanted was to study the habits of the dwellers in Nottingham in the fourteenth century, and spend a great deal more money on building houses on unliveable spots, which would cause him, in the future, as he told Osbert, to be known as "the great Sir George."

I was living in London when the first law-case began (there were three before the final débâcle). This was during one of the most appalling battles of the war. Osbert was with his regiment in the trenches. Sacheverell, too young to go to the slaughter, was at Eton.

The creature who had succeeded in involving my unfortunate mother, who was terrified at the size of her debts, tried to blackmail my father. When he did not succeed, he induced my mother (so frightened and bewildered by this time that she would have done anything which she was told would lift the fear closing in upon her) to allow it to be said in court that the whole squalid affair was the result of her wish to pay Osbert's debts, which amounted to less than £10, and which *he* paid.

Osbert came back on leave after one of the most terrible battles to find what had been done to him. That warm-hearted, chivalrous creature *pitied* her.

Old Sir George Lewis, the family solicitor, told him that he could go into the witness box and deny the monstrous slander, in which case she would be punished for that slander, or he could refrain from going into the witness box and endure the calumny, in an attempt to save his mother from what would have undoubtedly been the result of that lie.

"Then there is only one thing to be done," said Osbert. He did not go into the witness box, and allowed himself to endure that calumny.

As my mother was fond of saying, "There *is* such a thing as Duty."

This beautiful story of a mother martyrised for her son's sake roused a great deal of feeling. As Sacheverell's housemaster at Eton said to him, "It is a good thing a war is on, so that your brother can fight for his King and country—otherwise nobody would ever speak to him again."

CHAPTER EIGHT

Ticket-of-Leave Woman

There can be no doubt that, although they are to be pitied, my father and mother were not unmixed blessings to their offspring.

However, at about the beginning of the 1914–1918 war, I escaped from them for a short while, as a ticket-of-leave woman, since my father did not dare to allow me to remain at home for fear that the scoundrels who had succeeded in enmeshing my mother might entrap me into telling a truth which would enable them to blackmail him.

Therefore, under the chaperonage of Helen Rootham, then my governess, I took a small flat in Moscow Road, Bayswater, where I lived as best I could.

The flat was on top of a large building, and from this there was a singularly beautiful view of trees in Kensington Gardens. There were two sitting-rooms, and Osbert, poor as he was, gave us, whenever he came on leave from the Front, beautiful hangings to enliven these. Helen's sitting-room was hung with green and silver, mine with red and gold.

I lived there very quietly. I was poor, but, although undernourished, I was never hungry, as Helen was a clever manager.

At first I worked at the Pensions Office in Chelsea, for the wage of twenty-five shillings a week and two shillings war bonus. (This I did partly out of patriotism, partly because I had to earn the money in order to live.) I had to "sign in" at the office at nine o'clock every morning, so my breakfast, which consisted of porridge, home-made scones and jam, and café au lait, was naturally early. For luncheon, in order to avoid the smell of fat in the canteen and the chatter of the admirable hard-working people there, I walked to a large shop in Sloane Square and lunched off a cup of coffee and milk, and two rolls and butter. For supper, back in Pembridge Mansions, I had a really delicious soup made of meat-bones and white haricot beans.

When my father learned that I was working at the Pensions Office from nine till five, he was overwhelmed with alarm for fear that my slight curvature of the spine would give trouble, that a doctor would have to be called in, and *he* would be responsible for the fees. I must, therefore, resign from the Pensions Office immediately and must go, as spy, to a photographer's shop in Bond Street over which he had some kind of hold. My wages were to be the same as those I earned at the Pensions Office, but I was to have this advantage over my life there: I need not appear at the shop before ten o'clock instead of nine. I was to listen at doors, read private letters, and repeat, immediately, to my father any hints of "goings on" in the shop that I might have observed.

To my father's high indignation, I refused to enter into the espionage employment he had designed for me. Years afterwards, when Osbert was dining alone with my father at Renishaw, waited on by Robins, my father said to Osbert: "If Edith had done what I told her, she would be earning £1000 a year now."

This was too much for Robins. "Yes. But would she be getting it?"

"Leave the room, Robins."

When I came to London, I was unused to household work, but this ineptitude on my part was, gradually, cured. I am the crane-tall Jane of my poem "Aubade"— although, in the poem, I had changed my situation to that of a poor young country servant, resembling, perhaps, the young country girl in a wonderful picture by Modigliani that Osbert once owned.

The young country servant was looking out on an eternity of kitchen garden; I was not, but the auditory life, the visual life, the early-dawn life, were mine—the cockscomb-ragged hair was mine.

> *Jane, Jane,*
> *Tall as a crane,*
> *The morning light creaks down again;*
>
> *Comb your cockscomb-ragged hair,*
> *Jane, Jane, come down the stair.*
>
> *Each dull blunt wooden stalactite*
> *Of rain creaks, hardened by the light,*

Sounding like an overtone
From some lonely world unknown.

But the creaking empty light
Will never harden into sight,

Will never penetrate your brain
With overtones like the blunt rain.

The light would show (if it could harden)
Eternities of kitchen garden,

Cockscomb flowers that none will pluck,
And wooden flowers that 'gin to cluck.

In the kitchen you must light
Flowers as staring, red and white,

As carrots or as turnips, shining
Where the cold dawn light lies whining.

Cockscomb hair on the cold wind
Hangs limp, turns the milk's weak mind. . . .

> *Jane, Jane,*
> *Tall as a crane,*
> *The morning light creaks down again!*

Intellectual society was, at that time, divided into several camps, and to none of these did I, by nature, belong. On the one side was the bottle-wielding school of thought to which I could not, owing to my sex, upbringing, tastes, and lack of muscle, belong. On another side was the society of Bloomsbury, the home of an echoing silence. This section of society was described to me by Gertrude Stein as "the Young Men's Christian

Association—with Christ left out, of course."

Some of the more silent intellectuals, crouching under the umbrella-like deceptive weight of their foreheads, lived their toadstool lives sheltered by these. The appearance of others aroused the conjecture that they were trying to be foetuses. But to what rebirth and subsequent life they looked forward, I do not know. One intellectual lighthouse, as an American admirer called him, was immensely tall, and if he had not been so inert one would have supposed him to have been involved in a death-struggle with a lamppost. They seemed to be inextricably intertwined. From the top of this edifice from time to time a few dim sparks emerged, but they did not cast much light on anything.

In this world of superior intellect there were several models. There was, for instance, the amphibian model —with gaping mouth, glassy eyes staring at nothing in particular, and with a general air of slipperiness and, at the same time, scaliness.

There was, too, the village-idiot model, drooling, and with a boastful exhibition of mental deficiency—also the deliberately awkward and blundering good-sportsman-and-cricketer model.

The ladies of this world were not, to my mind, attractive. For the most part they had faces like fawn-coloured felt hats that had been inadvertently sat upon. They spent their time in chronicling the doings of the unexciting female chatterboxes of previous centuries— passed over by history (that terrible mill in which sawdust rejoins sawdust) and remarkable only because of their inexhaustible enthusiasm for dossing down in every ditch with every little frog disguised as a bull. On the borders of this society was a purely social agglomeration—one alien to the society in which I was brought up—a society which, using money as a battering-ram and broadmindedness as a weapon, brought off invasions of a world hitherto unknown to them. All these beings lived in the shade of certain powerful and protective persons, eminent and accommodating divines, sleek and pouting, filling their coats and own spiritual needs as completely and fully as a neatly rounded potato fits its skin, and leaders of society, some with voices like the bellowing of the golden (or brazen) calf, others like a tunicate, possessing, to quote the scientific description of this elementary form of life, a preference for dwelling amidst mud. A stomach and a mouth, but neither nerves nor a heart. To these were added some elderly peers and a few clean-shaven Americans, or pseudo-American business-women, possessed of large salaries and immense competence, who carried huge and expensive bags with gold fittings, from which they would produce what appeared to be time-tables, and whose voices, movements, and general habits gave the impression that they had portable homes situated on the platforms of Victoria Station.

I knew the painter and distinguished art critic Roger Fry well, for I sat to him for several portraits. For one of these I wore a green evening dress, the colour of the leaves of lilies, and my appearance in this, in the full glare of the midsummer light of midday, in Fitzroy Square, together with the appearance of Mr. Fry, his bushy, long grey hair floating from under an enormous black sombrero, caused great joy to the children of the district as we crossed from Mr. Fry's studio to his house for luncheon.

Imagining us to be strayed revellers, they enquired at moments (perhaps not unnaturally) if our mothers knew we were out. At other moments they referred to the 5th of November, a date dedicated to the memory of the activities of Guy Fawkes, when, according to them, our appearance would have been better timed.

Mr. Fry was a most delightful companion, learned and courteous; he had a great gift for attracting and retaining friendship. Warm-hearted, generous-minded, and kindly, he was always espousing some lost cause, championing some unfortunate person, rushing at some windmill with a lance. In other respects he was dreamy and vague, incapable of noticing any but a spiritual discomfort. I remember an incident when I was lunching at his house after a sitting. Mr. Fry's slippers could not be found anywhere, and a game of hunt-the-slipper ensued. In the midst of the fun, a loud crash was heard, and a hoarse voice said, "Coal, Sir!" "Put it, my good man—" said Mr. Fry, whirling round and round like a kitten chasing its tail, losing his spectacles, and speaking in a voice weak from fatigue—"oh, well, put it on the bed."

At this point I found the slippers in the milk-jug, and the fun stopped.

We were much in the company of Ada Leverson shortly after the time of which I write. She had been named "The Sphinx" by poor Oscar Wilde, to whom she had shown a goodness to be remembered, for ever, with gratitude. I do not know why he called her this, for there was nothing mysterious about her.

In appearance she resembled a very wise owl entangled in a bush of singularly thick, singularly bright forsythia. She bore also a strong likeness to Sarah Bernhardt in the latter's old age.

She could always be relied on for "le mot juste." On one occasion, looking at a young lady who was obviously afflicted with incipient nymphomania, she said to me, in a stage-whisper, "Oh, my dear, I have always so much preferred the bread-and-butter miss to the tartine." Referring to the same young lady, whose arms were in an unfortunate state of nudity from the shoulders downward (in those days arms were shrouded during the daytime), she enquired, in the same stage-whisper, and with a look of mingled bewilderment and horror: "Oh, my dear, do you suppose those are legs or arms?"

She could safely be left to deal with any situation. Called upon to accompany an afflicted mother in pursuit of an errant (and very rich) twenty-one-year-old son, who had fled to the Carpathians with a shop-soiled married lady twenty years his senior, her aid in dealing with the matter was invaluable. On their arrival at the hotel where the errant one was staying, he advanced to meet the ladies, exclaiming almost with tears, "Oh, what have I done, what have I *done?* We were walking in the mountains and an enormous black bear dashed from behind a rock, and I—ran away and left her."

"Poor beast," said Mrs. Leverson, drawing her furs

round her, and shuddering slightly. "I suppose it hugged her, and now she is blackmailing it."

The romance was at an end.

It was at this time that I got to know Nina Hamnett, one of the most generous people one could imagine. A bad writer has described her as a name-hunter. According to him, her generosity was extended to anybody who was somebody. I did not find this to be so. Nobody who went without to the extent that she did could be accused of doing so for the wrong motives. The cost is too great. If she had money, she invited her friends to share it with her. If she had no money, she had no food, unless friends were equally generous towards her.

She did not lack courage. Later on, in 1934, that black magician Aleister Crowley had Miss Hamnett, and of course her publishers, Messrs. Constable, up for libel. He lost his case, in the course of which he gave the following horrible evidence:

"The forces of good were those that had constantly oppressed me, I saw them daily destroy the happiness of my fellow men. . . ." He added that his magical experiments began in a flat in Chancery Lane. "I had two temples, one white . . . one black . . . a mere cupboard in which stood an altar, supported by the figure of a negro standing on his hands. The presiding genius of this place was a human skeleton . . . which I fed from time to time with blood, small birds, and the like. The idea was to give it life, but I never got further than causing the bones to become covered with viscous slime. . . . I expect," said Crowley, "that was the soot of London."

Although Mr. Crowley did his best to pursue an acquaintance with my brother and myself, I did not at the time wish to know him. But when, later on, I read about the sacrifice of a wretched cat, who was not properly killed during one of the obscene rites he practised, anger made me wish I had taken the opportunity. It would have given me pleasure to have said to him:

"Mr. Crowley, you will go straight to hell and you will meet only yourself, over and over again. Together with Lady ——, who, I hope, will talk to you."

Virginia Woolf had a moonlit transparent beauty. She was exquisitely carved, with large thoughtful eyes that held no foreshadowing of that tragic end which was a grief to everyone who had ever known her. To be in her company was delightful. She enjoyed each butterfly aspect of the world and of the moment, and would chase the lovely creatures, but without damaging the coloured dust on their wings. Whenever anyone present said anything pregnant, she would clasp her long delicate hands together and laugh with pleasure. In her own talk she always went straight to the point.

For instance, on the first occasion when I met her, at a dinner party given by Osbert and Sacheverell, she asked me, "Why do you live where you do?"

"Because I have not much money."

"How much money a year have you?"

I told her.

"Oh well, I think we can do better for you than that," she said thoughtfully.

However, nothing came of this project, and I remained in Bayswater.

That, I think, was as well. I do not think I should have "fitted into" the closely serried company of Bloomsbury. I was not an unfriendly young woman, but I was shy, and yet, at unexpected moments, was not silent—and silence was much prized, sometimes to the embarrassment of persons outside the inner circle of Bloomsbury.

I suppose I was always rather odd to look at, from a conventional point of view (and nothing was more unconventionally conventional than the company of Bloomsbury). Looking back on myself, I can see that I had an untidy elegance like that of a tall thin bird—and was a being who appeared to have but a few friends, a few snowflakes, perhaps, as I have said, and a small bough of early-flowering almond blossom.

The company of Bloomsbury were kind-hearted, and from time to time I entered it on sufferance.

Lytton Strachey was a major Bloomsbury idol of this time. I knew him but slightly, and don't like his work. Also, his letters to Virginia Woolf, now published, make me blush from head to foot, with the exclamations of "Oh deary Mary me!" and the enumeration of Countesses known and dimly related to them.

Visually, he made the impression on me of having strayed from the companionship of the kindly demons in the Russian ballet *Children's Tales*, who existed only in profile, and had long beards of gardener's bass (actually I think he saw the beings of whom he wrote, with the exception of Queen Victoria, in profile only, never full face). He seemed to have been cut out of very thin cardboard.

He wasted no words in conversation. A young and robust friend of ours, Constant Lambert, meeting him at a party, said, "You don't remember, Mr. Strachey? We met four years ago."

"Quite a nice interval, I think, don't you?" remarked Mr. Strachey pleasantly, and passed on.

Remembering to forget, or, as Groucho Marx put it, buying back an introduction, was a great self-protective feature of the time. It was said—I do not know with what truth—that Sir Jacob Epstein, finding the late Mark Gertler, the painter, at the Café Royal, said to him, "Gertler, do you remember the time when we were not acquainted?" Gertler said he had some dim recollection of this. "Let us go back to that time, Gertler," said the great man.

Epstein was not, like Percy Wyndham Lewis, a man of war. But once, two days after those gentlemen had had a verbal battle at the Café Royal—the subject being Mrs. Epstein, the sculptor's first wife—there was an "incident" in the revolving door of a picture gallery. The two adversaries, one of whom was going out, the other going in, finding themselves in adjoining compartments, stopped, glaring at each other, so that the revolving doors were immovable, preventing the crocodile of persons from entering or leaving.

"Now then," said kind old Mr. Walter Sickert, one of the aspirants for entry, "if you two military gentlemen will get a move on, perhaps some of the rest of us will have a chance."

"Some are born military, others have militarism thrust upon 'em," said Mr. Wyndham Lewis, through clenched teeth. However, both stopped glaring, and they went on their ways.

Epstein's face bore a certain resemblance to that of William Blake. Their eyes were of the same visionary look and were of the same shape, though the visions they saw were of a completely different order.

Walter Sickert had a sense of fun that could be disconcerting, as Wyndham Lewis found out when he went to dine with Osbert and Sachie at the same time as Sickert. Sickert invented a character supposedly out of one of Lewis's novels, and asked him at length about him. Lewis thought he would get the better of Sickert by carrying on the pretence, and a long conversation ensued about a character who never existed. Neither Lewis nor Sickert gave up.

Sickert, however, had a most kind and generous side to his nature. Elsie Swinton, a great friend of his, took me to see him when I was seventeen and so shy that my hands were glued to my sides. Elsie said, "This woman admires your pictures."

"Either she is mad or she is very intelligent," Sickert replied. "Which are you?"

"Mad," I said.

He was so delighted that he gave me a drawing. It is one of my treasured possessions and I have it with me now in my London house.

Sickert lived mainly in the country, but used to stay in a small hotel for men only at Covent Garden. When asked why he went there, he said, "I enjoy hearing the porters singing like birds in the early morning." One day he asked if he might break the rules and bring his wife to stay. The proprietor thought for a long time and said, "Very well, Mr. Sickert. But it *must* be your wife and it *must* be a holiday!"

My young friend Denton Welch was one who discovered his formidable sense of fun, as he recorded in the copy of *Horizon* which was his introduction to me.

My brother Osbert was the first of our family to read it. He came into my room one afternoon, laughing so much that for some minutes he was unable to speak. At last he held out a copy of *Horizon* in which were some pages describing a visit paid by a very young man, whose name we did not then know, to Walter Sickert, whom we knew very well. In a series of portraits of an extraordinary brilliance—portraits of the great painter, of his wife, of a visiting eccentric, and of the obviously charming, very alarmed, youthfully self-conscious boy himself—Denton described how he was persecuted and terrified by the great man, who, wearing enormous boots reaching to his knees—boots such as are worn by deep-sea divers—had insisted on dancing to him during tea (I suppose in order to see how Denton would react to the experience). As Denton left the house, Mr. Sickert said, "Come again—when you have a little less time."

CHAPTER NINE

Aldous and Maria Huxley

Among the first of our friends in London were
Aldous and Maria Huxley. We met Aldous for
the first time when we asked him to contribute to our
yearly anthology *Wheels*. He invited me to luncheon at
the Isola Bella—a restaurant in Soho—on a dreamlike
golden day in June. The air was like white wine,
spangled with great stars of dew and sun motes,
haunted by sounds like echoes of memories. In a moment, as I came out of this light into the cool restaurant,
the day seemed quenched by a sudden pleasant darkness
and by the silence of my host.

Aldous Huxley was extremely tall, had full lips and a
rather ripe, full, but not at all loud voice. His hair was of
the brown, living colour of the earth on garden beds. As
a young man, though he was always friendly, his si-
lences seemed to stretch for miles, extinguishing life,
when they occurred, as a snuffer extinguishes a candle.
On the other hand, he was (when uninterrupted) one of
the most accomplished talkers I have ever known, and

his monologues on every conceivable subject were astonishing floriated variations of an amazing brilliance, and, occasionally, of a most deliberate absurdity.

The animal and vegetable world became endowed, under the spell of his talk, with human characteristics, usually of a rather scandalous nature. I remember one monologue of this description on the subject of the morals of the octopus tribe—the tribe in question being, according to Aldous, conversant with Ovid's theory of love. He expatiated on the advantages possessed by the octopus in every amorous adventure . . . so many arms with which to enfold the beloved! His enthusiasm grew as he proceeded. We were, at the moment, on a platform in Sloane Square underground station. It was Sunday morning, the platforms were crowded, and the passengers waiting for trains listened, spellbound, to the monologue.

Another monologue dealt with the loves of the melon. No melon, apparently, was safe from the advances of another melon. Nor was there any prohibited degree of kinship. That was why gardeners kept them so closely under glass.

But these conversations sprang out of his lighter moods. At other times he would talk with my brothers on the subject of such painters, sculptors, and musicians as we had been ordered to despise by the older generations—artists who are now, once more, owing to a natural change of taste, in favour with the public: such musicians as Rossini, such sculptors as Bernini.

At this time I was a near neighbour of Aldous and his dear and lovely first wife, Maria, who had beautiful blue eyes like those of a Siamese cat, and a very endearing and gentle manner. When my brothers were away, we nearly always went to parties together.

Some of the parties were fun, others not. The parties of Lady X, the wife of an Emperor of Finance, held unexpected possibilities. Lady X was separated from the Emperor, but was expected to uphold his position. From time to time a message would reach her, borne by one of the discreet nation of secretaries to be found in the Emperor's house (confidential secretaries, business secretaries, financial secretaries, social secretaries), conveying Lord X's disapproval. Lady X was not spending enough money. More must be spent immediately. It was due to his position.

In a panic, Lady X would buy fifty gold cigarette cases and would shower these on the more impecunious of the young men of her acquaintance.

Then came the word: "The Arts must be patronised." This threw her into an even greater panic. How was she to patronise the Arts when she did not know which one, or even the name of one of the practitioners? Then she remembered.

An old Belgian lady had told her she had a nephew who was a poet. The very thing! The poet was imported. He was a terrible, very young man in a tulip-mauve suit, and he had large, liquid, over-expressive dark eyes. His verses were even more dreadful than he was. But they were very fashionable. This was in the early twenties, and to be in the fashion verses had to be printed in alternating lines of green, black, violet, and red. Some lines would read downwards (as in Chinese literature), a word per line, sometimes they would slant, from high on the right-hand corner to low on the left or, again, from low on the left to high on the right; but only very occasionally would they be printed plain, like mine.

Lady X saw, clearly, that he was exactly what she was looking for. At enormous expense she had the poems printed in a limited edition of five thousand on hand-made paper. But Lord X, by some sixth sense (for he had not seen the poems), divined that they were so terrible they must never be allowed to see the light of day. So he requested one of his secretaries (probably a confidential one) to repair to the publishers at crack of dawn on the day when the edition was to be sent for review and to buy up the whole edition. This the secretary did, at the same time hinting to the publishers that a terrible fate would inevitably overtake them if they did not fall in with the Business Emperor's wishes.

Lady X could not understand what had happened. Why were there no reviews? And why should the whole edition have been snapped up almost before the publishers' office opened? She ordered, quickly, a second edition. The same thing happened. It was a mystery! The third edition, the same!

After that, the history eludes me. But I think Lord X must have come to the conclusion that Lady X had better give the Arts a miss and give parties instead.

She did, and these were many (she was an extremely kind and hospitable woman). But the parties were a source of some terror to the younger among her guests, because their elders seemed always to be in a state of guerrilla warfare. Indeed, there were moments when a distinguished guest would arrive, catch sight of an alleged enemy, and vanish from the house before his hostess had received any indication of his entrance.

"Dear me!" I remember Aldous saying, sinking wearily into an armchair, just after we had received another invitation from Lady X. "What can we say *now?* Let me consider, please. How about Mr. and Mrs. Aldous Huxley and Miss Edith Sitwell thank Lady X for her last thirty-two invitations, which they regret they are unable to accept as all three are suffering from contagious epilepsy?"

A party to which I look back with great pleasure (although on this occasion, if I remember rightly, Aldous and Maria Huxley were not present) was given by a certain art critic, now dead.

He gave it in order to help an aging gentleman who had found himself in the plight of acting as publicity agent to a former artist's model who had decided, late in life, to adopt the career of dancer. (It is unknown for what reason.)

In a spirit of duty, Mr. Z, the publicity agent in question, had declared in a Sunday newspaper that Maharajahs were in the habit of pouring rubies into the lap of this lady in restaurants, and the hostesses were falling over each other to secure her services for their parties. But, as my brother Sacheverell said to me sadly, the only hostess who was really falling over himself was the art critic in question.

On the afternoon of the party, we were met on the steps of our host's house by the dancer, Mr. Z, and eleven young men with blond hair and long eyelashes who had been recruited from the chorus of a musical comedy and instructed to rush after the dancer like moths to a candle, to bend over her, and to exhibit signs of an almost insane infatuation and delight. Mr. Z was afraid, not without reason, that they might forget their instructions, so he told the drummer of the band to keep an eye on them and, if they flagged for an instant, to beat a furious tattoo.

All went fairly well until the dancer took the floor. To watch her was like watching a four-wheeler cab, heavily laden, leaving a station.

An old gentleman, sitting next to me, enquired in a loud voice: "What is she doing that for?"

Alas, like so many of Mr. Z's schemes, this one eventually faded out. But trying to be of use to Mr. Z was, at that time, in the nature of a national industry.

It is sad to think that our acquaintance ended as it did.

Mr. Z was, unfortunately, suddenly seized by an inspiration, and, prey to this, composed a drama which —so he assured my brother Osbert—was in blank verse and recorded the sufferings of those ill-starred lovers, Paolo and Francesca. This he insisted on Osbert reading. (We had not, at that time, developed our present virtuosity in dealing with senders of manuscripts.)

It was thought by my family that Dante had already chronicled these sufferings adequately, and that there the matter might have been left. But no, Mr. Z was adamant.

My brother sighed, put down the manuscript, and went for a walk. When he returned, the treasure, which was the size of the week's laundry in a station hotel, had vanished.

It was not until many months afterwards, on one of the infrequent occasions when both the cat and her offspring were absent from her basket at the same time, that it was discovered that the drama had been used to line this. Unfortunately, when found, the work bore not only evident traces that it had been subjected to the inevitable va-et-vient and general wear and tear attendant on the cat's frequent accouchements and nursing operations, but it looked, also, as if it had been torn by tigers.

My brother wished to have the manuscript retyped— but not a line was decipherable, and, had it not been for Dante, the fate of the ill-starred lovers would have remained for ever a mystery.

Then came the problem—how to tell Mr. Z the fate that had befallen his masterpiece, and the *reason?* The mind boggles, faced with such a situation!

Nature has supervened on our behalf, wrapping us in a blissful forgetfulness of the outcome of the matter. All we remember is that, from then onwards, our lives and the life of Mr. Z ran in different channels.

Aldous and Maria went to live, for a time, in Italy, then made their home in Hollywood. It was a happiness to me to see them again when I, too, spent some time there. Aldous was unchanged.

I remember one long drive to the house of a great astronomer living in the neighbourhood. Aldous oc-

cupied the time by moaning about the unfortunate
lapses of certain great poets of the past.

"Really, Edith, that a man like Coleridge, *presumed*
to be sane, could write:

> *"Why need I say, Louisa dear,*
> *How glad I am to see you here,*
> *A lovely convalescent!*
> *Risen from the bed of pain and fear*
> *And feverish heat incessant.*
>
> *"Believe me, while in bed you lay,*
> *Your danger taught us all to pray,*
> *You made us grow devouter!*
> *Each eye looked up and seemed to say*
> *How can we do without her!*

"And then there was Wordsworth:

> *"There's something in a flying horse,*
> *There's something in a big balloon.*
> *But across the clouds I'll never float*
> *Until I have a little boat*
> *Shaped like the crescent moon.*

"Really!"

CHAPTER TEN

Dining Out

O ne of my great pleasures at this time was dining out and I enjoyed, particularly, visiting the house of Sir Edmund and Lady Gosse, although the pleasure was not unmingled with terror, for one could never foresee exactly what Sir Edmund was going to do to one conversationally. His skill in this lost art of conversation was unbounded. It ranged from the talent of a musician, harmonious and exquisite, to that of a polished and urbane warrior. Never were there such ambushes, laid with such a certain and cunning hand; never were the tactics of the fleeing victim foreseen and forestalled more victoriously.

Sir Edmund and Lady Gosse lived, with their two delightful golden-haired daughters (Miss Sylvia Gosse, the painter, is one of these), in a house in one of the terraces of Regent's Park. The wall-paper and the whole house had a sort of 1870 brownness about it, the drawing-room was filled with a cheerful sound of tea-spoons, which seemed to haunt it even when tea was over or had not begun, and the house was crowded with treasures of all kinds; but no treasure was greater than Sir Edmund's conversation, nor was any treasure-seeking in the world more fraught with danger.

The house was ruled in part by Parker, the parlour-maid, a very famous character, and still more by Buchanan, a large black and white cat. Buchanan had apparently entered the house from some unknown place, and had taken over the charge of it. He would not come down to meals until the whole family was assembled in the dining-room, and, this being done, he insisted upon Sir Edmund mounting the stairs and ringing the dinner-bell. Buchanan would then walk downstairs, in a dignified way, and eat his dinner with the rest of the family. When teatime came, Buchanan refused, firmly, and without showing any signs of yielding, to drink his cream unless Lady Gosse, kneeling, held the saucer for him. If, as occasionally happened, he was indignant for some reason or another, he would leave the room, and an awed silence would fall. I remember one occasion when I was dining at the house and Buchanan left the room after dinner in a marked manner, Sir Edmund and Lady Gosse discussing, in a frightened whisper, all possible causes which could have given Buchanan offence. He had his own writing-paper and envelopes specially made for him, not too large, and when Sir Edmund went away on a visit, Buchanan would dictate letters to him every day (Lady Gosse told me in a whisper that she was afraid Buchanan was a sad gossip) and Sir Edmund would reply.

But this story begins, really, before the reign of

Buchanan. Osbert, Sacheverell, and I were in the habit of visiting the house as often as we dared, to indulge in the delights of Sir Edmund's reminiscence and Lady Gosse's and her daughters' great charm. Sir Edmund's memoirs of the pre-Raphaelite poets were an unending delight to us. There was, for instance, the story about William Morris visiting Rossetti's studio after having given him the poem about Sigmond. Rossetti thanked him: "But, my dear fellow," he continued, "I can't really take much interest in someone whose father was a dragon."

"I can't see it is any worse," replied William Morris sharply, "than being someone whose brother is a fool."

After that, the proceedings became misty as far as Sir Edmund was concerned, for he was very young and too terrified by the last remark and its implications to regain consciousness.

His stories, too, about the rows in the house in Chelsea which was shared by Swinburne and Rossetti were very pleasing, rows in which Swinburne would throw himself on to the floor and scream in a horizontal position, and Rossetti would remain stiffly upright, with his arms raised above his head, and scream in a perpendicular position. The rhythm of the two screamers was, apparently, flawlessly interwoven, the noise like that of an express train.

But these were the delights, and not the terrors, of Sir Edmund's conversation, and now we must examine the darker side of this.

On one occasion, when I visited the house, I found a Swedish gentleman whom Lady Gosse informed me was the greatest living Swedish poet, "and," in a whisper, "his poems have never been translated into English; but he understands English perfectly." Sir Edmund, at this point, pounced upon me and said in a loud voice: "Come over here, Edie, and tell him . . . how much you enjoy his poems." The Swedish gentleman beamed. After five minutes of moral anguish on my part, Sir Edmund pounced again: "Don't stand there looking so dull and awkward, Edie. You make me feel quite cross and naughty." This was a favourite phrase of his.

Sir Edmund felt cross and naughty, for instance, on the occasion when, terrified at having to call at the house after an absence of nearly a year, I induced Siegfried Sassoon to come with me, in the hope that he might avert the nemesis which I knew to be awaiting me. "And if," I said, "Sir Edmund Gosse drags me to a secluded corner, Siegfried, I shall be obliged if you will kindly come too, otherwise I shall be torn to bits."

Sir Edmund beamed at me on my arrival, and said: "Now, Edie, let us come over to this quiet corner and have a talk."

Siegfried followed the execution procession, looking very determined, whereupon Sir Edmund turned on him and demanded in a taut voice: "What are *you* doing here, Siegfried? We don't want you, I'm sure! We are not talking about horses. You make me feel quite cross and naughty!"

But one of my most alarming experiences in this very delightful house was a dinner party which was graced by the presence of Mr. George Moore.

Mr. Moore had not, I think, arrived in a very happy

frame of mind; and this state was aggravated by the conversational habits of another guest. At first Mr. Moore remained steeped in an impenetrable gloom, but after a while he turned to me and, in a voice shaking with indignation, hissed: "Yes, yes, yes, forty million thousand yes's. How *can* I talk when someone says yes, yes, yes?"

To this question, no answer could be returned, so I remained silent. Afterwards Mr. Moore relented so far as to speak of a most interesting book called the Bible, which contained the intimate history of a most interesting people, the Jews, and, as well, to inform me that he had discovered there was a vehicle called an omnibus which would take one to any destination, should one be fortunate enough to attract its attention. As we left the house, Mr. Moore perceived one of these vehicles, and rushed towards it, crying, "Omnibus! Omnibus!" But, alas, he was not fortunate on this occasion, and did not attract the attention of the omnibus, which went on its way without him.

CHAPTER ELEVEN

The Missing Collar

It was, I believe, in the year 1921 that I first met that involuntary recluse Mr. Percy Wyndham Lewis.

It would be ridiculous to deny that Mr. Lewis was a very considerable writer. If he were not so completely jaundiced that all colours, good and evil, seemed to him as one, he would, indeed, have been a great one. But persons who either have not read Mr. Lewis or have not read Jonathan Swift are in the habit of confusing the nature of their gifts. These are of an entirely different order.

Swift was incapable of lying, and his hatred was the reverse side of love. Swift feared nothing and nobody. Lewis enjoyed lying, not only as a defence behind which he could hide, but as an idol. It may be said that what he himself called Cato's truth, or the expedient lie, was his god. "If you don't use the lie, it is as if you made war upon a nation armed with bombs and gas with flintlocks or just with fists."

There are men who seem to have been born without relations but with a collar, and Lewis was one of these. He remained immured in this faithful friend, and I think it must have figured on his passport. Certainly one had only to add up the rings on it (made by time), as one adds up the rings on a palm-tree or on the horns of an antelope, to arrive at some estimate of his age.

Mr. Lewis visited us at Renishaw, but this visit, alas, was not entirely happy, for he mislaid his collar on the morning after his arrival, and could not come down to luncheon until he had found it. But eventually Robins, Osbert's delightful ex-soldier servant (by this time butler at Renishaw), tracked it down, and it flapped back on to Lewis's neck, much as a weary and rather dilapidated blackbird might return to its nest.

This temporary parting of the ways in Osbert's house caused Mr. Lewis, after three years' brooding on the subject, to believe that Osbert, Sacheverell, and I are evil symbols of the decay of civilisation, and to denounce us in a book called *The Apes of God*—God being, in this case, Lewis, although the only resemblance between that gentleman and his creator lay in both having brooded over chaos.

Before the collar calamity I sat to Lewis for the portrait of me that is in the Tate Gallery, and also for several drawings. But, in the end, his manner became so threatening that I ceased to sit for him, and his portrait of me, consequently, has no hands.

His studio was situated in a piece of waste ground off Kensington High Street, haunted by pallid hens, squawking desolately and prophetically; and the appearance of Mr. Lewis's hair aroused in some observers the conviction that the feathers of these had sought within its shades a refuge from the general confusion. Another school of thought, however, ascribed the alien substances by which it seemed to be bestrewn to a different cause, believing them to be a sprinkling of the snows of time. For the nature of his toilette, and his general appearance, undoubtedly aroused attention and gave rise to speculation.

His complexion, always dark, was at moments darker than others; and this pigmentation was due to no freak of nature or chance, but to habits and choice. His clothes seemed as much a refuge as a covering, and when fully equipped to face the world and the weather, he presented much the same appearance as that which we are privileged to see in photographs of certain brave men at the very moment of their rescue after six months spent among the polar wastes and the blubber.

His outward personality, his shield against the world, changed from day to day—one might almost say from hour to hour. When he grinned, one felt as if one were looking at a lantern slide . . . a click, a fade-out, and another slide, totally unconnected with it, and equally unreal, had taken its place. He was no longer the simple-minded artist, but a rather sinister, piratic, formidable Dago. For this remarkable man had a habit of appearing in various roles, partly as a disguise (for caution was part of his professional equipment) and partly in order to defy his own loneliness. For in this way so many different characters inhabited his studio (all enclosed in his own body, so that they had no opportunity of contradicting him or paying him insufficient attention and homage) that he had scarcely any need of outside companionship. He had to appear in different roles in order to impress himself, and, if possible, others.

There was the Spanish role, for instance (to which I have referred already), in which he would assume a gay, if sinister, manner, very masculine and gallant, and deeply impressive to a feminine observer. When appearing in this character he would wear a sombrero and, from time to time, would allow the expression "Carramba!" to escape him, and would build castles in the air (or prisons for the objects of his affections) with square blockish movements of his thick meat-coloured hands. (Foreigners gesticulate.)

Then, when, as was invariably the case, the castles in the air and the prisons did not materialise, he would abolish them again with a single stroke. He would, too, when out of doors, draw his stick along the railings, with what he hoped was a flash of teeth. But always, just as the teeth were about to flash, the sun went in, so that the phenomenon was not observable, or his shoe-laces came undone and he was forced to do them up, so that the people on the top of the passing omnibus who had been intended to witness and to admire the flash could not see it. His life was full of little disappointments of this kind.

At other times he would appear in a nautical role, shooting short sharp sentences through his clenched teeth in a bluff hearty voice, much as the captain of a whaling schooner would issue commands in the teeth of a gale to his crew—rough diamonds to a man, but with

114

hearts of gold, and obviously adoring their skipper.

It was interesting to observe his demeanour when he attended a party. Advancing towards his hostess with a business-like abstraction, totally ignoring his feet—not in the least rudely, but as one ignores old and tried friends who can be trusted to do their best for one—he would shunt his right arm towards her as if it were a set of trucks, and thrust his hand in hers with much the same movement one might use in disposing of an unwanted parcel, liable to come undone at any moment.

His life was overshadowed by real, or imaginary, dangers. He was, for instance, a prey to the conviction that Roger Fry and Clive Bell roosted, permanently, on the roof of his studio, in order to observe his slightest movement. Then, too, there either were, or were not, the rats. At one time Mr. Lewis got it into his head that these were lurking amidst the confusion.

"D'you mind rats?" he enquired of me one day. I said that I did. "Well, they're here, all right," he said. "Night and day. Day and night. But I'll try to keep them off." With which he gave a swish to his brush and went on painting.

Personally, I think a certain Gargantuism in his outlook exaggerated the size of mice into that of rats. As time went on—according to subsequent sitters—the mice, unhampered in their activities, grew bolder. They would loll against the furniture and stare in a most insolent manner, and when a certain distinguished poet was sitting to Mr. Lewis, they actually went so far as to climb on to his knee and scrutinise his face in what seemed to be a disapproving fashion. So at last Mr.

Lewis was driven to buy a large gong, and when their behaviour became quite intolerable, he would bang this at the opening of the mouse-hole. They would then retreat.

Not only Mr. Lewis's life, but that of his sitters was fraught with dangers. For all the objects in his studio whisked past one at such a terrific rate, propelled by some unseen force (or, perhaps, by the hope of escaping), that one was never sure what one was stepping on.

From time to time Mr. Lewis would give a savage kick to the varying and warring objects which hid the floor from view and which seemed (when not trying to escape) to spend their whole time in clamouring for his attention, so that he frequently presented the appearance of a harassed mother returning home with her wearied and quarrelsome offspring after a particularly noisy Bank Holiday.

Mr. Lewis produced a book of somewhat bewildering verse, *One-Way Song*. It is more than a little difficult to disentangle the central themes in this—as difficult, indeed, as to distinguish the events chronicled in this verse

> *They told me you had been to her*
> *And mentioned me to him,*
> *You gave me a good character*
> *But said I could not swim.*
> —Lewis Carroll

and in the rest of that well-known poem. One thing, however, appears very clearly in Mr. Lewis's verse, and

that is that *somebody* had been behaving pretty badly—
had not been kind.

Now, Mr. Lewis, in spite of his boyish playfulness, in
spite of that Boy Scout movement for elderly Boys
called "The Enemy," in spite of being, as you might say,
a Regular Pickle, had a strong vein of sentimentality
underlying all his brusqueness. Just as in that long
plaint *The Apes of God*, in the midst of worrying about
the wickedness of those who did, or did not, accept
invitations to luncheon, tea, or dinner, live in studios, or
pretend to be young, he could yet find time to long for
the hero, Mr. Pierrepoint, to be not only feared but
loved, so in *One-Way Song* Mr. Lewis longed for his
friends to love him, he longed to be understood. (Oh,
would not *somebody* be kind?) This sentimentality,
masquerading as brusqueness, grew to such a pitch that
we are reminded, in both books, of an early nineteenth-
century Junges Mädchen counting the petals of a mar-
guerite, pondering over the last words, the last look, of
the Herr Leutnant, and longing, oh more tenderly than
anyone will ever, *ever* know, for him to turn from those
wild ways of his and appreciate true worth!

More often still, we are reminded of a dear old lady
howling denunciations of this person and of that, making a scene and "creating," as the servants say, because
the Vicar no longer appreciates her church work now
that he has taken up with those *horrid* minxes who are a
third of her age and have thirty times her attractions
("Lor, Miss Pipchin, love, how you do create, to be
sure! Now you sit down and have a good rest and a hot
strong cup of tea, and then you'll feel better!"). But Mr.

Lewis *would not* rest! He rejected the strong cup of tea and, egged on by such Powers and Portents as Mr. Montgomery Belgion and his equals, he created, yelling defiance at those who did, or did not, issue or accept invitations to luncheon or dinner, underrate their ages, or live in studios.

According to his own account, the creations in *The Apes of God* were received by a shower of mingled bouquets and brickbats. His life was, he assured us (Enemy Pamphlet No. 1, Satire and Fiction), threatened by an Airman.

In *One-Way Song* we find Mr. Lewis in a gentler mood. Who, he seemed to enquire, could be more amenable, was more formed to be loved?

> *I'm not too careful with a drop of Scotch,*
> *I'm not particular about a blotch.*
> *I'm not alert to spy out a blackhead,*
> *I'm not the man that minds a dirty bed.*
> *I'm not the man to ban a friend because*
> *He breasts the brine in lousy bathing-drawers.*
> *I'm not the man to baulk at a low smell,*
> *I'm not the man to insist on asphodel.*
> *This sounds like a He-fellow, don't you think?*
> *It sounds like that. I belch, I bawl, I drink.*

In spite, however, of those soft allurements, in spite of all those endearing young charms, Mr. Lewis, according to himself, was not appreciated, though he even went so far as to apologise for any little brusqueness that might have been noticed.

> *I'm sorry if I've been too brutal, girls.*

We tried to reassure him. "Now, Mr. Lewis, not another word, please. We beg! You know, you ought not to spoil them. And, besides, the pretty dears like your caveman stuff! For it is not often that they meet a real He-man . . . and when they do . . . !"

Much of *One-Way Song* is occupied with Time, which Mr. Lewis held in great fear.

"I am thirty-seven till I pass the word round," he said to us on one occasion. "D'you understand?" This got on my nerves to such an extent that when told by a doctor to say "ninety-nine" I responded, invariably, "thirty-seven."

In this poem, however, we have Time as a metaphysical concept, not as an enemy of another kind, and we find Mr. Lewis putting down his foot very firmly on one matter:

We must be frantically frontal,

he told us, and we were warned about what would happen if we were not. He suffered from various little troubles that he would have liked us to understand and to sympathise with, apart from the trouble about backs and fronts, and this, at moments, grew to such a pitch that he scarcely seemed to know if he was going or coming.

Try and walk backwards: you will quickly see
How you were meant only one-way to be!
Attempt to gaze out of your bricked-up back:
You will soon discover what we One-ways lack!
Endeavour to re-occupy the Past:
Your stubborn front will force you to stand fast!

119

No traffic-caption of Sens Interdit
Is necessary for this clearly One-Way Street.
Address yourself to sitting down front-first—
Your joints will stop you, or your hips will burst!

(Oh, will not *somebody understand?*)

Again, we tried to reassure him—telling him that he
was amongst *friends*, who would stand by him. The
situation described by him, we knew, must have been
most trying. But these little things would occur, and we
begged him not to fret about the seriousness of the
symptoms.

Mr. Lewis's pictures appeared, as a very great painter
said to me, to have been painted by a mailed fist in a
cotton glove.

The novels are crammed with Gargantuan distortions
of Mr. Lewis's own character, which yet threatened his
existence, so that we are reminded of Swift, in his last
illness, threatening his image in a mirror.

Poor man! The only real fault in him was an un-
conquerable suspicion of everybody who admired his
great potential gifts, seeing in that admiration a plot to
gain his confidence and then hand him over to his real or
imaginary enemies. He longed, I think, to be liked, and
would have been by everybody; but he simply did not
know how to receive affection. My two brothers were
faithful friends to him, I was loyal to him in the teeth of
a good deal of opposition. He repaid us and the others
who had been inflexibly loyal to him in *The Apes of*

God. In this, incidentally, he more than hinted that I am a woman of infamous moral character. He was reproved for his attack on me, in a letter from Mr. W. B. Yeats, who, in addition to the reproof, wrote that I had brought back into literature "a quality absent for a generation and rare in the literature of all ages, passion ennobled by intensity, and by wisdom."

CHAPTER TWELVE

A Man with Red Hair

I wish I could remember in what year, when my brother Osbert and I arrived at Montegufoni on a visit to our parents, we were greeted by my father with the news that "a most extraordinary man came over to luncheon here—a man with red hair: I think he is a writer; he said his name is Lawrence. He had heard of you. He brought his wife. She jumped on all the beds after luncheon—to see if the mattresses were soft." (My father had a superb collection of painted and gilded seventeenth-century beds.) "When they signed their names in the visitors' book, she put, after hers, 'Geborene,' and then something I couldn't read. So extraordinary! *Of course* she was born! Everybody is."

(The visitors' book was a source of incessant bewilderment to my father, as strange entries made, from time to time, their appearance. Once, for instance, after a peer with two titles, "So-and-So and So-and-So," had lunched, my father found written, directly under this entry, that of

Swan and Edgar
Waring and Gillow

—the names of famous London shops.)

A few days after we received the information about
the visit to Montegufoni of Mr. and Mrs. Lawrence, we
received from them an invitation to tea.

We drove through the Tuscan countryside to their
tall pink house, that looked as if it were perched upon a
hen's legs. It was full of Lawrence's pictures. The
subjects of these were rather like a solid Doppelgänger
of Mrs. Lawrence, and made one feel as if one had been
very severely bumped! Otherwise, the house had a
serious continental comfort. Mr. Lawrence looked like a
plaster gnome on a stone toadstool in some suburban
garden. At the same time he bore some resemblance to a
bad self-portrait by Van Gogh. He had a rather matted,
dank appearance. He looked as if he had just returned
from spending an uncomfortable night in a very dark
cave, hiding, perhaps, in the darkness, from something
which, at the same time, he on his side was hunting.

His hair, which had been very red, was now dimmed
by illness, as though dust, or ash, had quenched that
flame. It hung down, at moments, into his bright and
eager eyes, hindering him from seeing anything. He had
a sad look of illness; at times he had a kind of eager
quickness, as if he were afraid of something being left
unfinished. At other moments he would lag behind in
the conversation as if he was trying to drag time to a
standstill.

Though courteous and amiable, he was determined to

Care Of   [12]

impress upon us that he was a son of toil (that was the great romance, apart from his marriage with Mrs. Lawrence, in his life) and he seemed to be trying to make us uncomfortable by references to the contrast between his childhood and ours. But this was not our fault. Our childhood was hell, and we refused to be discomfited.

Mr. Lawrence talked to us a great deal about our parents, ascribing to them characteristics which were completely alien to them. They were, he explained, madly in love with each other, whereas the only times when they stopped quarrelling and thwarting each other were when they joined together to persecute their offspring.

Poor Mr. Lawrence had a very bad chip on his shoulder. He hated men who were magnificent to look at. He hated men who were "gentlemen."

At about the same time when we visited him, or soon after, he wrote *Lady Chatterley's Lover*, to me a very dirty and completely worthless book, of no literary importance, and unworthy of the man who could write "The Snake" and "The Mountain Lion"—two beautiful and most moving poems. In *Lady Chatterley's Lover* his loathing for Sir Clifford Chatterley amounted practically to a mania. Sir Clifford was so criminally offensive as to be a Baronet, and he, with most men, fought like a tiger in the first world war, instead of remaining safely at home, fornicating and squealing, shrilly, about the oppressions from which he had suffered.

Sir Clifford was also in trouble for being a famous writer. Fame should be left to persons behaving like the denizens of Monkey Hill at the zoo.

The book contains certain remarkable faults of taste, as when Mr. Mellors, the adulterous gamekeeper, speaking of his master, who had been desperately injured in the war, said, "He as good as told me I was a disreputable character who walked about with my breeches buttons undone [nothing could have been more true] and I as good as told him he'd nothing to unbutton anyway. It's not for a man in the shape you're in, Sir Clifford, to twit me for having a cod between my legs."

Nobody seems to have thrashed Mr. Mellors, which was what he deserved, and this unutterably filthy, cruel, and smelly speech has been, apparently, accepted by the more idiotic of the British public as being a fine example of the workingman's frank splendid mode of expression. No decent workingman, no decent man of any class, would have uttered it. It is an utterance worthy of Monkey Hill.

My respect for the olfactory sense and that of my readers prevents me from quoting Mr. Lawrence's enthusiastic descriptions of Mr. Mellors' sexual equipment. However, at one time there was a disappointment; Mr. Mellors' equipment did not come up to expectations. But there was a compensation. The nasty little nymphomaniac he had got mixed up with was able to wreathe their treasure with forget-me-nots!

I do not think the four-letter words in this book are as harmful as the descriptions of sexual intercourse, which in my opinion would freeze any impulse to love between boy and girl.

The Times Literary Supplement of June 29, 1962,

reviewing Jean Rostand's *Bestiaire d'Amour* as translated by Cornelia Schaeffer, said, "He discusses violent caresses in slugs, seductive behavior in crustaceans, a few seconds of abandon in silkworms, the plumpness of a female toad's thighs and so on. Mr. Rostand's choice of words seems to be deliberately sensual throughout."

This might have been written of *Lady Chatterley's Lover*.

So much for one point of view.

Mr. Rupert Furneaux, however, in the distinguished seventh volume of his *Famous Criminal Cases:* "Readers may like to be reminded of the famous review of the American edition which appeared in *Field and Stream:* 'Although written many years ago, *Lady Chatterley's Lover* has just been reissued by the Grove Press, and this pictorial account of the day-by-day life of an English gamekeeper is full of considerable interest to outdoor-minded readers, as it contains many passages on pheasant-raising, the apprehending of poachers, ways to control vermin, and other chores and duties of the professional gamekeeper. Unfortunately, one is obliged to wade through many pages of extraneous material in order to discover and savor those sidelights on the management of a midland shooting estate, and in this reviewer's opinion the book cannot take the place of J. R. Miller's *Practical Gamekeeping.*' "

As I have said, I think the work worthless as a work of art. And I can only apply to it a five-letter word which, until Mr. Lawrence made a pet of it, was only allowed by our cricket-loving, golf-loving, tennis-loving compatriots to be used in connection with those games—not in connection with the game that interested Mr. Lawrence.

But to return to the tea party. Part of the conversation consisted in Mrs. Lawrence explaining the natives of Bloomsbury to me—sometimes correctly—and telling me how she had been obliged to protect Lawrence from the snares they laid for him.

The couple can never have had a dull moment, since everyone who met them fell in love either with Mr. or Mrs. Lawrence. All were potential seducers, and the utmost ingenuity had to be exercised in order to circumvent their plots. They had mercy on neither age nor sex. Anything might happen at any moment and in any place, and although it never *did* happen, that did not spoil the fun.

We did not see Mr. and Mrs. Lawrence again, for although there had not been time for us to fall in love with them, the fact that we had not done so turned us, automatically, into textbook cases, and our relations became strained, to say the least of it.

As a result of the trouble, I, when lecturing at Liverpool, said that Lawrence was the head of the Jaeger school of literature, since he was hot, soft, and woolly.

Messrs. Jaeger protested mildly. "We *are* soft," they wrote to me, "and we *are* woolly. But we are *never hot*, owing to our system of slow conductivity."

I replied, begging them to invent a system of slow conductivity for Lawrence, adding that I regretted having made the comparison, since their works are unshrinkable by Time, whereas the works of Mr. Lawrence, in my opinion, are not.

CHAPTER THIRTEEN

The Hours I Spent with Thee, Dear Love

There was a considerable turmoil when both the ex-Queen of Ruritania and the Comtesse de B— the ex-beautiful ex-friend of an ex-Monarch in a good social position (to quote the late Sir George Lewis's description of a certain Duke)—wished to come to luncheon with us on the same day.

"We can't have them together," my mother said.

"Why not?"

"*Why not?* One never knows."

Finally, we arranged that the ex-Queen was to come on the day she had suggested, and Madame de B on the day before this event. On Madame de B's day, shortly before one o'clock, the courtyard of the castle was filled with a brazen roaring like the bellowing of the golden calf, and in stampeded a bold buccaneering woman with strong legs. She was accompanied by her husband. There was no incident of any note at luncheon, but after luncheon Madame de B drew me aside and took up my character.

This, I am afraid, did not prove satisfactory.

"It is rare," she said, "to find a woman making her own life. Frankly, it is *not understood*."

A slight pause.

"Then you really put *this poetry* above Human Love?"

"Not as a Profession, Madame de B."

After La Belle qui fut Haulmière had departed, we had a rather peevish discontented rest, in preparation for our fresh troubles on the morrow.

"Their Majesties," the lady-in-waiting had written to my mother, "will be glad if you do not invite a large party to meet them." So we had a quiet luncheon party alone with the Queen and the ex-King, the lady-in-waiting and a gentleman-in-waiting. The Queen was a gentle faded woman, with black woollen stockings and wonderful pearls.

"Your daughter has not shingled her hair," she said to my mother.

"No, Ma'am."

"That is right. That is good. That is as it should be. It is the first question I ask of every mother: 'Have you allowed your daughter to shingle her hair?' From that I deduce everything, ah, everything."

Short pause.

"Your sons are not here."

"No, Ma'am."

"But they do not polish their nails? No?"

"No."

"*That* is goo-o-ood. That is as it should be. Of a young

129

man, I ask always, 'Does he polish his nails?' and when I am told 'No,' I say, 'That is good.' From that I trace that all is well."

Luncheon passed quickly on the wings of such conversation as this and an exciting discussion about past, future, and present Christmas cards, given and received.

"I like your English fashion," said Her Majesty.

"Yes?"

"But one must not be carried away. One must choose always something with some reference to the season, to the giver and receiver. Last year, for instance, my dear daughter-in-law had a card printed with a thrush sitting upon a spray of lilac, and underneath it the inscription 'If Winter Comes,' after the title of that delightful English novel that we all enjoyed so much. But I thought it a mistake."

"It is very artistic, no doubt," I said to her.

"But, my dear child, is it in keeping with the season?"

After discussing Christmas cards, we talked about the Queen's brother's collection of stamps, and after that, about scores at croquet.

Then the King said to me, "I am told that dogs have been known to pine if their masters go away. My dog likes me, or seems to. Do you think he would pine if I went away?"

I said that this would be highly probable.

After a little he enquired: "You paint, don't you?"

"No."

"But you should learn to paint, and then execute a

130

portrait of a dog after its master has gone away."

At last the day drifted into a long lacquered afternoon!

My life then, as now, was plagued with interruptions, much more tiresome than this one, because less fun. I could pass an examination about the corn that afflicted my Aunt Naomi in the year 1902. . . . In London interruptions were not only frequent, but seemed as interminable as they were unnecessary.

These much-lamented occurrences began to kidnap my time when I lived at Pembridge Mansions. As follows:

Extract from weekly paper: "Miss Sitwell, looking more hieratic than ever, like John the Baptist in a Chelsea drawing-room . . ."

Scene: Miss Sitwell's sitting-room in Pembridge Mansions. Hieratic woman lying on a sofa, fountain-pen in hand:

"The Gardener was old as tongues of nightingales
That in the wide leaves tell a thousand Grecian tales."

Enter Mrs. Young, my daily maid, a delightful warm-hearted Irish woman—a war widow: "You're wanted on the telephone, Miss."

Hieratic Woman: "Tell them I'm dead, Mrs. Young. Tell them to leave a message."

Mrs. Young (reappearing): "He won't go, Miss. He says it's important. It's Mr. Muggleby Lion. He says he can't leave a message. He'll ring up later."

Hieratic woman relapses. An hour's peace. Hieratic woman mutters: "a thousand Grecian tales"

Mrs. Young enters: "It's Lady Bandbox, Miss. She must speak to you on the telephone."

Hieratic Woman: "Oh, tell her to go to . . . Did you tell her that, Mrs. Young?"

Mrs. Young: "Yes, Miss. . . . Of course I didn't say exactly *where* she was to go, but I certainly left it to her imagination."

Hieratic Woman: "Tell her I'm in my bath, or I'm dead, and the funeral is tomorrow."

Mrs. Young: "Certainly, Miss." (*She returns.*) "Lady Bandbox says she *must* speak to you yourself, Miss."

Hieratic Woman rushes to the telephone and shakes it vigorously: "Yes! What *is* it? WHAT *IS* IT?"

Voice at the other end: "You *must* come to the Guru's lectures, darling. They're too marvellous! All about the Fourth Dimension and Numbers. If you add 4 to X and take away 9, you arrive at the letter F, the root number of the world. And then the *exercises* we do! We stand on one leg and put our heads under our arms, and when the blood rushes into our heads we are in the full state of Awareness and the Cosmos is just round the corner, and we rush to it and rebound right into the Fourth Dimension. . . . It's just as clear as daylight. And then, to continue about numbers. . . . It's too wonderful, we shan't be at sixes and sevens any more, he says, but it will all be threes and fives, and that makes such a difference to one's life—especially threes."

Hieratic Woman (*with ominous calm*)*:* "Yes, I know. Like the three balls outside a pawnbroker's shop."

Lady Bandbox (*delighted*): "Exactly, darling. . . . That means. . . ."

Hieratic Woman (*breaking away*): "Wine, Women and Song, very often!" (*Returns to the sofa, thinking:* "I'll not try to *write*. I'll just polish what I've got.")

Half an hour's calm.

Enter Mrs. Young: "Mr. Muggleby Lion is back again, Miss."

Hieratic Woman (*beside herself*): "Not *again*, Mrs. Young!"

Mrs. Young (*sympathetically*): "I'm afraid so, Miss. It really is too awful."

Hieratic Woman: "Damn his eyes, Mrs. Young." (*Pause*) "Did you tell him that?"

Mrs. Young: "Yes, Miss. At least I wrapped it up. But I certainly conveyed it. I said, 'You don't have to put up with Miss Sitwell's temper, Sir. I do.'"

Hieratic Woman (*subdued*): "I'm afraid so, Mrs. Young."

Mrs. Young (*gently*): "I think you'd better answer the telephone, Miss. He won't go away. Or if he does, he'll be back."

Hieratic Woman (*rushing madly to the telephone and shaking it as a terrier shakes a rat*): "What *is* it, Mr. Muggleby Lion?"

Fatuous Voice: "I must see you!"

Hieratic Woman: "*Why?*"

Fatuous Voice: "Well, there is something rather important. I might say, *very* important."

Hieratic Woman: "I am in the middle of working at a poem, Mr. Muggleby Lion."

Fatuous Voice: "I *hate* to interrupt you, but it is very important, so I'll come round this afternoon, and wait till I can see you." (*Rings off.*)

Mrs. Young: "Luncheon, Miss." (*Half an hour later*) "Letters."

Hieratic Woman (*opening one at random*): "This is from an American gentleman." (*Reads end of letter.*) " 'And I tell you truly, it is incense, incense, all the way. For you have been familiar with the Muses.' "

Mrs. Young (*shocked to the soul—crimson in the face with rage*): "I never did! Incest indeed! To my young lady, and *familiar!* He'd better come around here!" (*Pause*) "Oh, there goes the bell." (*She goes to the door, and returns, says gloomily:*) "Mr. Muggleby Lion, Miss."

Mr. Muggleby Lion: "I hate to disturb you, but I have just finished a *Little Sonnet*, that I *must* read to you."

Hieratic Woman (*coldly*): "It can't be a *Little* Sonnet, Mr. Muggleby Lion. Sonnets are all of the same size."

Then, of course, there is the post. . . .

It is seldom that a day goes by without some aspiring poet wanting me to pass judgment on his or her life work, or some chatty housewife regaling me with events of the *Mrs. Dale's Diary* variety. Then there are the letters from lunatics. These are my special delight. I have even been known to answer them. I choose a few examples at random.

A letter from an aircraftsman aged twenty: "I know

little or nothing of your own poetical career, I know only that you are a poetess," he said. "Every poet must have his or her critic. Whether the advice be taken or not is purely a matter that concerns the poet himself." He and his friends, he said, "strive against the virginity of morality"—whatever that may mean. Nor do matters stop there. "I have tried, during the last six or seven years, to express the inexpressible, to bridge the gap between mortality, to *become God!*" (The italics are mine.) "It is a difficult and dangerous life to follow. In doing so I have, perhaps, robbed myself and the world of intercourse. This saddens me and I am often given to abandoning poetry, but my life is already dedicated; there is no turning back."

I was naturally, in my humble way, rather overawed by the above, and did not know how to answer.

A few evenings after, I received a letter from a lady living in Croydon—also unknown to me, and also a genius. I forget now what she wanted, excepting that I was ordered to put down my work and flourish the banner of her genius before the multitude. "With Stravinsky and Tortellier and Prokofiev we have the movement starting," she wrote. "But these people are not universal enough and therefore cannot be bothered with anything outside their sphere. I am just the opposite with so much energy that 2,000 sketches, 3 dozen pictures, a good 20,000 words in articles and 10,000 for my fourth novel, plus my large picture, letters, and several dozen poems, hundreds of designs, etc. *all in eight months* [the italics are mine] *still leave me frustrated* for more work."

I am not exaggerating.

Because I did not answer her call to action within a week, the lady wrote me a violent letter accusing me (a) of being jealous of her genius, and (b) of being jealous of her fame.

Then there was a Mrs. X, who wrote to me from Aberdeen (I had just published two poems in *The Listener*).

> *Dear Dame Edith Sitwell,*
>
> Your recent poems in *The Listener* brought to my mind Dorothy Perkins, a niece of my brother-in-law the Reverend Alf Perkins of Glasgow whom I met while visiting there. (I was her Scotch Aunt Jessie, at that time Mrs. Hobson.) I recollect that she had just returned from a visit to you. Now my purpose in writing to you is to find out if you are still in touch with her. If so, let me have her address, and write to her to ask her to communicate with me.
>
> She once met me at Lincoln Station, and took me to stay with her at her home in Lincolnshire.
>
> If you are not in touch with her, kindly trace her.
>
> *Yours sincerely,*

At that moment I was nearly yelling with frustration, since I had a great deal of work to do and was prevented relentlessly from doing it. I wrote:

> *Dear Madam,*
>
> I have notoriously nothing to do, therefore furnishing the address of somebody of whom I

have never heard fills in my time pleasantly.

Still. . . .

Which of my two poems in *The Listener* reminded you of Miss Dorothy Perkins? One poem was about a high yaller girl, the other about an old lady who had been a member of the oldest profession in the world.

I have never even heard of Miss Dorothy Perkins, let alone met her, so she can hardly have visited me. I have never heard of the Reverend Alf Perkins of Glasgow. Quite frankly, I do not care if you were, or were not, Miss Perkins' Scotch Aunt Jessie, or if you were or were not Mrs. Hobson at that time. Nor do I care if Miss Perkins did, or did not, meet you at Lincoln Station, or if she did, or did not, take you for a holiday at her home in Swallow. Why do you not ask the Reverend Alf Perkins for his niece's address, instead of bothering me? He must, surely, be more able to give you this than someone who is a complete stranger to the whole lot of you.

Yours sincerely,

P.S. Since writing the above, I have been told that Miss Perkins was last heard of at Mitylene, where she was working for a Mr. Bolt.

I received this final letter from the genius from Croydon:

Dear Madam,

I would be obliged if you would kindly return both my Creation text and my two letters sent to

you a few days ago. Whilst Jordan and Mr. Holt
Molesly and Picasso bleed the public for evil I must
literally beg on hands and knees to be allowed to
help the people regain their serenity. I had thought
you'd be big enough to help but your energy is obviously on the wane.

Awaiting your reply.

P.S. Are you afraid to be eclipsed by genius when
your mundane art stagnates itself in Art and not
in Life?

P.P.S. If I am bitter—why not? I do more in one
day than others *in 1 year and no one sees*. Or is
greatness born of inspiration too lofty for you to
achieve?

CHAPTER FOURTEEN

The Audience Is Meant to Laugh

I t was in 1922 that I wrote *Façade*, the then much-derided poems for which nobody else is in the least to blame. William Walton and I were in closer collaboration than is usual when poems are set to music, because he was then sharing a house with my two brothers. The idea that we should collaborate originated with them, and the first performance took place privately and peacefully at their house in January, 1922.

But in June, 1923, the first *public* performance, at the Aeolian Hall, was anything but peaceful. Never, I should think, was a larger and more imposing shower of brickbats hurled at any new work. These missiles have now been exchanged for equally large and imposing bouquets. But at that time there was not a bouquet to be seen. Indeed, the attitude of certain of the audience was so threatening that I was warned to stay on the platform, hidden by the curtain, until they got tired of waiting for me and went home.

Certain newspaper critics, enraged and alarmed by the performance, rushed from the hall and, lassoing a passing postman, asked him what he thought. Dashing back to the hall, they waylaid a fireman and anxiously asked his opinion. These modern substitutes for the Delphic Oracle replied promptly, and in no uncertain terms. They opined that we were mad.

This coincided, of course, with the opinion of the critics, confirmed and strengthened them. I hope I shall not be accused of casting aspersions on the culture of the critics, the postman, or the fireman. I am not. All I am saying is that they were precipitate in giving their opinion—spoke too hastily, as did other custodians of aesthetic tradition and the purity of the English language.

At the time I began to write, a change in the direction, imagery, and rhythms in poetry had become necessary, owing to the rhythmical flaccidity, the verbal deadness, the dead and expected patterns, of some of the poetry immediately preceding us.

Rhythm is one of the principal translators between dream and reality. Rhythm might be described as, to the world of sound, what light is to the world of sight. It shapes and gives new meaning. Rhythm was described by Schopenhauer as melody deprived of its pitch.

The poems in *Façade* are, in many cases, virtuoso exercises in technique of an extreme difficulty, in the same sense as that in which certain studies by Liszt are studies in transcendental technique in music:

*Thetis wrote a treatise noting wheat is silver like
the sea; the lovely cheat is sweet as foam;
Erotis notices that she . . .*

Because I could write that work it was assumed that I
care nothing for the state of the world and the misery of
my fellow-men—that I am eccentric and a heartless fool,
and that I am incapable of writing anything but works
such as *Façade*.

This opinion was pronounced widely, constantly, and
in violent terms. But, there again, the people who ex-
pressed this opinion were precipitate in giving it. I have
since written other poems.

And it has now at last dawned on these people that
Façade is a work for the most part of gaiety, although
sometimes there is a veiled sadness. The audience is
meant to laugh. It has dawned on them, too, that the
work is utterly devoid of malice, and of the stupid and
vulgar trick known as leg-pulling. And that the old
accusation that we were trying to gain self-adver-
tisement by the use of a megaphone is absurd. We
used it, at the suggestion of my brother Sacheverell,
who stage-managed the performance, because otherwise
the voice of the speaker could not be heard above the
music.

And now for the poems. As I have said before, they
are in many cases exercises in transcendental technique.
"Fox Trot," "I Do Like to Be Beside the Seaside," "Sir
Beelzebub," "Something Lies Beyond the Scene," the
"Waltz," and the "Hornpipe" are examples. Many of the

poems are jocose, in the same way as that in which Stravinsky's *Chansons Plaisantes* are jocose—but they are, none the less, serious from an aesthetic point of view.

One reason for the misunderstanding that arose round these poems is the fact that they are abstract patterns— in the sense in which pictures are sometimes abstract patterns. Monsieur Cocteau, writing of a work of the same kind, said: "For the majority, a work cannot be beautiful without a plot involving mysticism or love. . . . Beauty, gaiety, sadness without romance are suspect."

The technical experiments in these poems consist, for the most part, of enquiries into the effect on rhythm and on speed of the use of rhymes, assonances, and dissonances placed not only at the end of lines, but at the beginning, and in different and most elaborate patterns throughout the verse, and, too, there are enquiries into the effect on speed of equivalent syllables. By this I mean that if you use one three-syllabled word, it has a greater speed than the three one-syllabled words which might have been used as its equivalent. The use of two rhymes placed immediately together at the end of each of two lines sounds like leaps in the air.

"Sally, Mary, Mattie, what's the matter, why cry?"
The huntsman and the reynard-coloured sun and
  I sigh.

Other experiments were made to discover the effect on rhythm of thickening and thinning, sharpening and softening, consonants, as in certain lines of the "Waltz":

142

> *The stars in their apiaries,*
> *Sylphs in their aviaries . . .*

These are followed by lines which end sometimes with a dissonance, sometimes a rhyme:

> *Seeing them, spangle these, and the sylphs fond,*
> *From their aviaries fanned*
> *With each long fluid hand*
> *The manteaux espagnoles,*
> *Mimic the waterfalls*
> *Over the long and the light summer land.*

In this poem, the waltz rhythm is produced by the use in the first lines of two-syllabled rhymes *beginning* as well as *ending*, the lines

> *Daisy and Lily,*
> *Lazy and silly,*

followed by two long lines with assonances:

> *Walk by the shore of the wan grassy sea—*
> *Talking once more 'neath a swan-bosomed tree.*

There was great trouble with the critics about those two lines, just as there was trouble about the "reynard-coloured sun" and the "pheasant-feathered corn" in the "Fox Trot." Has nobody seen a red-gold autumn sun, or walked near a cornfield? "A wan grassy sea"? Is not the sea often the colour of summer grass? "A swan-bosomed tree." Has nobody seen a tree covered with snow?

Some of the poems appeared to have a violent exhilaration, others have a veiled melancholy, a sadness masked by gaiety.

Their apparent gaiety caused them to be suspect. They were useless. They were butterflies. They were spivs. And yet I cannot but remember that when the great seventeenth-century naturalist John Ray was asked "What is the use of butterflies?" he replied "To adorn the world and delight the eyes of men, to brighten the countryside, serving like so many golden spangles to decorate the fields." And he added, of these butterflies made by the hand of God, "Who can contemplate their exquisite beauty and not acknowledge and adore the traces of divine Art upon them?" At least these poems made by the hand of Man may have the traces of human art upon their wings.

CHAPTER FIFTEEN

Eccentricity

It was during this time—as well as before and after-wards—that I met many people who have come to be regarded as "eccentrics."

The study of what constitutes eccentricity is, to me, a fascinating one. It is a many-sided study, involving also that of genius and of what constitutes aristocracy of the mind and of behaviour.

Eccentricity is *not*, as dull people would have us believe, a form of madness. It is often a kind of innocent pride, and the man of genius and the aristocrat are frequently regarded as eccentrics because genius and aristocrat are entirely unafraid of and uninfluenced by the opinions and vagaries of the crowd.

J. S. Sargent, a most charming and kind man, might well have claimed to be the chronicler of the eccentrically ordinary world, in which everything must be hidden, yet seems to be exposed to view.

"I cannot see the man for his likeness," Virginia Woolf quotes Roger Fry as saying of one of Sargent's truth-hiding verisimilitudes. "First, the collie dog which the Duke caresses has one lock of very white hair; secondly, the Duke's boots are so polished that they glitter; thirdly, the Duke's collar is very large and very stiffly starched; fourthly, the Duke was, when he stood for his portrait, sunburnt. After that we might come to the Duke himself." But by that time Mr. Fry was so "deadened by the fizz and crackle of Mr. Sargent's brush work that [he could] see nothing."

"Fizz and crackle." That was the outward sign of this intense ordinariness.

But there were delightful exceptions. One was Roger Fry himself, who did not care in the least for public opinion but was always gloriously himself. I have related elsewhere how (in post-Edwardian days) this great critic and earnest-minded painter would rush, slithering on his knees, at a hundred miles an hour, holding a paint-brush in his hand, along a strip of wall-paper spread on the ground, pausing only to admire the results brought about by the paint-brush, or a spilt cup of coffee, or the design made by his dog having sat down on the wet paint. "Really, *rather* an interesting effect," he would say.

A superb instance of *real* eccentricity was the late Lord Berners (Gerald to his friends). He was in full flower in later reigns, but his beginnings were in the reign of King Edward. His eccentricity was the result, as was Squire Waterton's, of a sheer sense of fun. He had a superb power of retort, which his adversary would, in self-defence, ascribe to eccentricity.

One of his acquaintances was in the impertinent habit

of saying to him "I have been sticking up for you." He repeated this once too often, and Lord Berners replied, "Yes, and I have been sticking up for you. Someone said you aren't fit to live with pigs, and I said that you are."

A pompous woman of his acquaintance, complaining that the head-waiter of a restaurant had not shown her and her husband immediately to a table, said, "We had to tell him who we were." Gerald, interested, enquired, "And who were you?"

On one occasion when my brother Sacheverell, my sister-in-law, and I were lunching with Gerald, his stately, gloomy, immense butler Marshall entered the dining-room bearing a huge placard. "The gentleman outside says would you be good enough to sign this, my Lord."

Gerald inspected the placard and wriggled nervously. "It wouldn't be any use, Marshall," he exclaimed. "He won't know who I am—probably has never heard of me."

It transpired, eventually, that the placard was "An Appeal to God that We May Have Peace in Our Time."

Mr. H. G. Wells comes into the category of an eccentric, appearing in this character not because of any remarkable habits or predilections, but rather because of his intense and eloquent ordinariness. He may in justice be claimed to be the figurehead and spokesman, the glorified quintessence of Strube's Little Man—his worries, his fears, his love of liberty and of fair play, his defiance of authority, are the same. But with this differ-ence: that, unlike the hero of Strube, Mr. Wells had a very large and carefully arranged brain and an extremely useful, if not very exciting, power of communicating his ideas in writing. Words, we may say at this point, seemed to interest Mr. Wells mainly as a means of communicating *ideas*, not in any sense as a means of evoking beauty or of producing beautiful sound. To my mind, a writer should not block out the possibility of any one of these desirable results of the skilful use of language. However, to continue.

Mr. Wells was intensely English; no other country, to my belief, could have produced him—not even Germany, though he has a Teuton's earnestness, varied by playfulness. Just as, in spite of the efforts of German architects, it takes an Englishman to produce our garden cities and the type of intellect contained therein, so it took the English landscape and mentality to produce Mr. Wells, and there are moments, indeed, when one feels that, if it be true that certain cities of the ancient world were built to the sound of music, it must be equally true that the garden cities of the present age arise from the sound of Mr. Wells's voice. There is a peculiar kinship between them.

That high-minded man John Galsworthy also qualifies as one of these super-ordinary eccentrics because of his curious habit of gloating over the aristocracy, and his almost maniacal addiction to the Old School Tie.

I met him once only. Dr. Meyerplatt, a kindly and industrious German Jew who had translated works by Wilde, Mr. Galsworthy, and other eminent English writers, was visiting England at the time of this meeting, and he made it a point of honour to bring Mr. and

Mrs. Galsworthy face to face with my brothers and me. Rather, I imagine, against her husband's will, Mrs. Galsworthy invited us to dinner. Strongly against my will, knowing, as I did, that Mr. Galsworthy had, quite mildly and kindly, denounced me as a writer about "cocky-ooly birds" (whatever these bipeds may have been), I accepted. My brothers were unable to do so, but Mrs. Galsworthy was forced by the industrious Doctor to issue a second invitation, which Osbert was able to accept. I forget why Sacheverell was not; possibly he was out of London.

Our hosts were kind and hospitable. Nothing occurred during my visit, excepting that Mr. Galsworthy, for the most part, looked through me as if I was transparent, and, at other moments, staring fixedly at my very large forehead, obviously lamented this phenomenon as an advertisement for brains in women.

I admire Mr. Galsworthy's novel *The Man of Property* greatly, differing in this, I believe, from most of my exact generation of writers. I persist in thinking it to be one of the best records of the suffering of youth that has ever been written (resembling, in this way, that far greater book *Anna Karenina*).

Nobody with any heart could fail to be moved by Mr. Galsworthy's true nobility of spirit, his constant defence of the weak and suffering, and his compassion for the poor. Nor can we cease to be grateful for the fact that we owe it to him, I believe, at least in part, that solitary confinement in prisons was abolished.

The following, therefore, is more a portrait of the age of King George the Fifth than one of the man who always battled for the right *as he saw it*. (I have never been able to understand how he did not recognise the cruel, the disgusting treatment of the girl June by that arch cad Bosinney—who was, after all, his invention—in *The Man of Property*.) He seemed, indeed, the epitome of the gentle, stern revolt of the age of King George the Fifth against the overblown cupids, coronets on table linen and bed linen, emulating Heavenly Crowns, of the reign of King Edward the Seventh.

Mr. Galsworthy looked, in some way, like the statue of an Elder Statesman. I do not know if he ever wore a frock coat (as he saw himself, I think, as a country squire), but this form of dress seemed to be his spiritual home. Had he ever been able to relax into a dressing-gown, he would have borne some resemblance to the figure that the cautious Mr. Sherlock Holmes placed as a target for the evil attempts of Dr. Moriarty and others. He would certainly have been moved into a fresh position by some unseen agency every quarter of an hour, in order to present some semblance of life. His face was like that of an old-fashioned solicitor. It had that peculiar calm which, to my mind, is rarely to be seen on any face save that of a member of this highly respectable profession. (I may say that *our* solicitors, who are also our personal friends, are addicted to an innocent form of "joyosity.") Mr. Galsworthy, however, unlike old-fashioned family solicitors, did not wear side-whiskers, but was closely, even secretively, clean-shaven. One felt that if he had been called to give evidence, his client need not fear that any damaging fact of importance would be presented in any but the most favourable light.

150

(This would be especially true if the Honour of a Little Woman was in question. "I think we are all Harrow men here," said the squire in *The Country House* on some such occasion. Of the Honour of Little Women I will speak later.) Mr. Galsworthy had a strange obsession about Patricians (as he called these social phenomena). Indeed, in the most innocent way, he seemed to be a Baronet fetichist. This took the strongest forms in *The White Monkey* and *The Silver Spoon.*

The vulgar little Fleur, daughter of Soames Forsyte, was married to the eldest son of a 9th Baronet whose children had the curious habit of addressing him as "Bart." Fleur's baby son was referred to, inexorably, as "the eleventh Baronet." However, Baronets and future Baronets knew their place.

Marjorie Ferrers, the granddaughter of a Marquess, could not be turned out of Fleur's house when she was heard poking fun at her hostess to another guest, during a party; and her grandfather, Lord Shropshire, was addressed by the 9th Baronet as "Marquess."

Mr. Galsworthy seemed to have a nervous fixation, also, on the subject of monocles, for these seemed to him to be an outward and visible sign of the aristocrat. In moments of stress, of social insecurity, he relied on one for this reason. He did suffer, however, with the sight of one eye. His devoted friend and biographer Mr. R. H. Mottram tells us in his book *Some We Loved* an interesting anecdote of the occasion when, as a youth of twenty, he dined with Mr. Galsworthy at an hotel in Norwich. "I forget," he wrote, "what detail of the service it was that caused him to assume his monocle and

speak with authority to the waiter. I know that it commanded instant attention."

This was the use of the monocle. Here is another
which we owe to the same authority. "Any slight to Ada
[Mrs. Galsworthy], any attempt to be too friendly with
his dog, an over-charge on a cab fare, would suddenly
bring something formidable to the surface. His monocle
would drop, the blue-grey became steel-grey, the jaw
would suddenly usurp the massiveness one had attributed to the brow, and he would say, with delibera-
tion, something so curtly annihilating that he would
have to break off with a light laugh at the consternation
he had caused." "An overcharge on a cab-fare." No
doubt, like the rest of us, he did not care to be taken for a
fool. But many times in his letters we find references
(*not* put forward by himself as a proof of his goodness,
not as a charity, but as a matter of course) to his great
generosity.

Mr. Galsworthy exercised remarkable restraint with
his much-loved friend Edward Garnett when the latter
told him that the beings in *The Patrician* were drawn
without intimacy and produce the effect of guess-work
done from outside. This was preceded by "You don't
know these people well enough."

A hard blow! Mr. Galsworthy reminded his "dear
boy" that he had always "suffered a little from a sense of
injustice" at his hands—ever since he read an extract
from Mr. Garnett's report on *Jocelyn* ("which should
never have been sent to me") "to the effect that I should
never be an artist but always look at life through the
windows of a club."

Furthermore, in another letter Mr. Galsworthy wrote: "As to knowledge of these people. Well, how can you tell—in the first place, you don't know them yourself; in the second place, after all, half my set at Oxford belonged to them. . . . Believe me, there is not the vast gulf between them and ordinary (!) people that you imagine." The exclamation mark is Mr. Galsworthy's.

But Mr. Garnett persisted in his missionary efforts. "Honestly," he wrote in a letter dated September 21, 1910, "the effect of much of the class atmosphere of *The Patrician* on me was that of an outsider writing of people he couldn't be intimate with, and *yet* was *familiar* with"! ! The friendship, however, continued.

At this time, as I have said, the good names of Little Women had to be protected. This was sometimes a little difficult, owing to the behaviour of these ladies.

Amongst these obstructionists was Lady Angela Forbes, a bad hang-over from the Edwardian era.

This household pest strongly resembled—in colour, figure, and profile, and, in general, an impression of tattered hairiness—an elderly gorilla afflicted with sex-appeal. In her autobiography, which she was so unwise as to publish, she proclaimed that I was "the despair of a good-looking mother," and that Sacheverell, then a schoolboy, was—I forget what adjective she applied to him, but one adjective was the same to her as any other—a nasty little boy "who never spoke in words of less than three syllables."

I forget what I replied about myself to the newspaper that quoted these attacks. But apropos of Sacheverell, I reminded the readers that "Angela" is a word of three syllables, yet that this was of no account in the case in point, as all the young males of her acquaintance referred to her, invariably, by words of one syllable—one Biblical, the other veterinary. Angela Forbes was, in some ways, the epitome of the Edwardian reign, and in that age everything seemed inflated, more highly coloured than life, with enormous roses, pink as the Gadarene swine who swarmed in the gardens.

Vulgarians whom I will not allow to intrude upon my private life are in the habit of saying and writing that I am an "eccentric."

As I have said, all artists and aristocrats are eccentric inasmuch as they are not in the least afraid of the crowd. I am eccentric only inasmuch as I do not suffer fools gladly and I am adamant in refusing to allow ignoramuses to teach me the spiritual and technical side of the art which I have practised for nearly half a century. I am always willing to learn, but I prefer to learn from teachers who know what they are talking about, and whose knowledge of technical proficiency equals mine. My would-be teachers complain that I lack simplicity, whereas nobody ever born was more simple. By simplicity they mean what Roger Fry called "an empty and mechanical simplicity—a simplicity [that] does not emerge from a profound feeling for harmonising the complexities, but is imposed violently upon it, everything being reduced to a bleak geometrical regularity and uniformity."

In the delightful television series *Brothers in Law*, founded on a novel by my friend Henry Cecil, a barrister, speaking of a judge before whom one of his friends was doomed to appear as counsel, said: "He makes Genghis Khan seem like Godfrey Winn."

This is exactly the light in which people who do not know me, regard me. Whereas, in private life, I am an extremely mild person.

CHAPTER SIXTEEN

The Turkish Army Put to Flight

My life at Pembridge Mansions, which had begun by being so delightful though poverty-stricken, had now become increasingly difficult. Helen Rootham had produced the best translation of Rimbaud's *Les Illuminations* that I know. She had every right to be proud of it. I had worked at disentangling the various versions of Wilfred Owen's war poems (sometimes almost indecipherable from the mud of the trenches smeared over them). Siegfried Sassoon, when he was obliged to go to the United States, had left them in my charge.

But then, suddenly, life rotted. Helen, a wonderful friend to me when I was a child and young girl, seemed to become semi-poisoned by the smell of money and a silly wish to "get into society." She and her sister (when the latter paid a visit to Pembridge Mansions) sprouted into such high super-lineage that it became obvious to me that they were absentees from the *Almanach de Gotha*. In short, they were not so much wishing to get into society as enthroned there. They were very grand, and the grandeur blew up almost to bursting point.

Helen was also much obsessed by dreams, or perhaps I should say "visions." There was one that interested her profoundly. She saw two Beings, lying side by side. Suddenly, out of one Being issued something that might have been a huge leaf, or might have been a great flame of fire, and this deliberately entered the other Being.

What *could* it mean? There must, obviously, be *some* meaning, and she had determined to find out what! She would, therefore, give full details to all the young males of my acquaintance, and enquire, "Do you know what it means?"

They said that they did.

Helen had made great friends, towards the end of the first war, with various refugee Serbs or Croats, and these told her that in a previous existence she had been their Princess Yellena, who, single-handed, had thrown the Turks out of wherever they happened to be at the moment.

This made her unusually troublesome (a) because she realised that she was really a Princess (this she had always known subconsciously), and (b) because every single human being she saw became, automatically, the advancing Turkish army and had to be repelled. She became extremely watchful. Anybody who spoke to me and did not confine their entire attention to her must, necessarily, have criminal instincts, otherwise for what reason could they possibly wish to speak to me?

Having already had an operation for the tragic illness from which she later died, she decided she would like to go to Paris to live with her sister, who had relinquished the house in London. Two things helped to make up her mind for her. The rent for our flat was raised and the atmosphere of the neighbourhood lowered. The street on which we lived was much haunted by a gentleman with gorilla-coloured hair and his two assistants. One day I opened the door and found the gorilla-coloured man standing on my threshold. He put his foot in the door and suggested that I come with him to see his little baby who was "so very pretty." I stamped on his foot and he retired, howling. After this I locked my door carefully. A few days later the manager of the grocery shop in a parallel street opposite was found murdered and nobody in the district saw the three men again—except, perhaps, the murdered man.

Helen and I left for Paris.

My life there was unmitigated hell. I did not mind, in the least, carrying the "boîte à l'ordure" downstairs every night. But I *did* mind the open accusations of wickedness, and the threats that I was going mad. "Have you looked at yourself in the glass?"

Poor Helen! She had been so good and kind when I was a child and very young girl, and I shall never forget that.

Her death was very terrible.

The two people whom I remember with pleasure from this unhappy time are Gertrude Stein and the painter

Pavel Tchelitchew, to whom she introduced me. Gertrude was verbally very interesting, the more so as she invariably got everybody wrong. She looked rather like an Easter Island idol, was immensely good-humoured, and had a remarkable ability to work in the midst of any amount of noise. She had been known to sit in a garage while her motor was being repaired, writing with complete concentration. But she did not suffer fools gladly. Her salon, for which she was famous, was divided. Gertrude talked to the husbands, it was the job of Alice B. Toklas to entertain the wives and the less interesting of the guests. Sometimes it became apparent to the guests that they had been divided thus, and repeated attempts were made on their part to do something about it. Miss Toklas, however, remained firm.

I was, I am glad to say, always put next to Gertrude! It was at my invitation that she came to England later on to lecture in this country.

Her work is an illustration of the success and also of the dangers of revolution. She is the last writer in the world whom any other writer should take as a model; but her work, for the most part, is very valuable because of its revivifying qualities, and it contains, to my mind, considerable beauty.

"These artists," said Roger Fry in his catalogue to the second Post-Impressionist Exhibition, "do not seek to imitate life, but to find an equivalent for life. . . . In fact they aim not at illusion but at reality. The logical extreme of such a method would undoubtedly be the attempt to give up all resemblance to natural form, and to create a purely abstract language of form. . . ."

This seems to me applicable to Miss Stein, with her extremely strong visual sense, strengthened, no doubt, by her friendship with the most important painters of her day.

She said to me, in one of our conversations, "The difference between Picasso and inferior painters is that inferior painters put in all the leaves on a tree, with the result that you see neither tree nor leaves. Picasso paints one leaf upon a tree, and you see the life of the tree."

She threw a word into the air, and when it returned to the ground it bore within it the original meaning it bore before custom and misuse had blurred it.

"If we look at an isolated printed word," said William James in *Principles of Psychology*, "and repeat it long enough, it ends by assuming an entirely unnatural aspect . . . its body is indeed there, but its soul is fled. It is reduced, by this new way of attending to it, to its sensational nudity. We never before attended to it in this way, but habitually got it clad with its meaning the moment we caught sight of it, and rapidly passed from it to the other words of the phrase. We apprehended it, in short, with a cloud of associates, and thus perceiving it, we felt it quite otherwise than as we feel it now, divested and alone."

This, I think, is at once the danger and the value of Miss Stein's method. The value is that she does show us the identity of words, deprived of their old smothering associations. Of course, every accomplished writer does this to some degree. But Miss Stein goes further than most writers. At the same time, we see objects afresh.

160

The child and the great artist—these alone receive the sensation fresh as it was at the beginning of the world.

I intend to give the barest outline of the life of Pavel Tchelitchew, that tragic, haunted, and noble artist—one of the most generous human beings I have ever known.

Tchelitchew was born on the 21st September, 1898. He was a member of the ancient Russian aristocracy, whose family had for centuries been attached to the Imperial Court. His great-grandmother was a daughter of the Sultan of Turkey and the Sultana (not the child of a member of the harem).

Tchelitchew's father was a man of liberal outlook, but the fact of his strongly held views on the subject of the distribution of land rights to the peasants did not destroy his loyalty to his Czar. Nor was his son's noble passion of grief at the sufferings of the poor, of the hungered—a real anguish that we see in many of his drawings, such as that of a ragged destitute boy lying sleeping happily in the warmth of the sun—to change his loyalty towards the Imperial family whom his ancestors had served.

Owing to their liberal views, the Tchelitchew family would probably have remained unmolested at the time of the Revolution. But they were aristocrats, and so must share the fate of their class. All the family properties and money were seized, leaving them entirely destitute.

In the autumn of 1918, the family left Moscow for

Kiev, where Pavel's beloved elder half-sister and her husband had a large estate. But there, as elsewhere in Russia, food was extremely scarce—indeed, as Mr. Soby said in his book on Tchelitchew, almost unobtainable by thousands.

From Kiev, Tchelitchew made his way alone and penniless to Turkey, where he endured the extremities of poverty. Eventually, while there, he joined a Russian travelling theatre, painting their scenery in return for being allowed to sleep on the stage, and sharing with the company the potatoes and bars of chocolate which were their only food.

By slow degrees he moved to Berlin in the autumn of 1921, where his work was received with enthusiasm. The Berlin State Opera commissioned him to do the sets and costumes for Rimsky-Korsakoff's *Coq d'Or*, produced in 1923.

In that year he went to live in Paris, and here it was that Miss Stein, having seen a small picture of his, "burgled," as she told me, from his very poor studio in the Boulevard Montparnasse, when he was absent. On his return, he found that not a single work remained. The burglary accomplished, Miss Stein paid for the lot.

She did everything possible to help him. But his desperate poverty continued, yet he shared everything he possessed, his meagre food, with those who were as poor as himself. He was the most generous man I have ever known, a wonderful friend, and tireless in thinking of ways in which to help others.

The only real danger in his nature was that he was

taken in by anyone who flattered him, and he was surrounded, therefore, by insignificant persons of an unfortunate kind. The women were, on the whole, more tiresome than the men. "Il y a quelque chose étrange en elle," he would say about every new discovery. Whereas the only thing that was "étrange en elle" was a lethal boringness and an incapacity to behave herself.

I sat to him for six portraits (one, at the Tate Gallery, is the property of Edward James). He executed, also, a sculpture of my head in wax on wire, one of his three only sculptures. This head of me is in America; but I own one in the same medium called *The Clown*, a most tragic work which is, actually, a self-portrait.

Tchelitchew, his dear and lovely sister, Choura (Madame Zaoussailoff), with whom he lived in Paris (she made the tragic, laughing, beautiful Anna Karenina a living human being for me), and I became great friends. This, I may say, did not prevent us from having rows of an unprecedented ferocity. Indeed, several times, according to him, my life was in imminent peril.

For instance, there was one terrible Saturday afternoon at a time when Tchelitchew had taken a studio in London. The floors were particularly slippery. I was sitting to him for one of his portraits of me. Suddenly, a storm of a particular violence blew up—I do not know, have never known, for what reason, ascribing it, however, to the fact that he had hurt one of his toes the day before and, although I was absent at the time of this misfortune, attributed it to some carelessness of mine.

In any case, he took to hurtling the armchair in which

I sat across the slippery floor as if it were a peram-
bulator, at the same time uttering shrieks of rage and, at
moments, hurling bare canvases past my head, being
careful, however, that they did not hurt that organ.

"Yes, yes, I choos [just] *keel* you, you know! I choos
keel you."

"Very well, old boy," I said, resigned to my fate. "If
you must, you must! But kindly respect my amber!" I
was wearing the enormous amber ornament which figures in his portrait of me at the Tate Gallery.

He had locked the door and put the key in his pocket.
The anxiety then arose—it being a Saturday, it was
impossible to summon the aid of a locksmith—as to
whether I must remain locked in the studio until Monday, or be rescued by the police or fire brigade. It would
have been difficult to summon these, as my chair was
whirling across the floor at lightning speed, far from
the telephone, and the situation, even if I had succeeded
in reaching the telephone, might not have been understood.

However, suddenly footsteps were heard ascending
the stairs, and Cecil Beaton's voice penetrated the
clamour (he was coming to tea with us).

Shaking the door violently, he shouted, "Oh, what *is*
happening? What *Is* Happening? Open the door *at
once*, Pavlik, do you hear me? Open the door!"

"For heaven's sake, Cecil," I screamed. "Stop shaking
the door. He has got the key in his pocket, and if you
shake the door, the lock will break, and I shall be here
till Monday. And, Pavlik, stop shrieking."

He did, and said calmly, "That must be Cecil coming

to tea." We had a nice quiet tea party, and no reference was made to the storm.

Usually, after these outbreaks, when both had been extremely angry, he would say, "Now, no more crossings, please." At one time he would not speak or write to me for four years, because, he said, I was a great friend of a certain Café Society Duchess. (I had never even seen the woman!) But in the end he forgave me, and our friendship was resumed.

He was, at times, wildly funny, both in his letters and in conversation, usually on purpose, sometimes inadvertently. For instance, having been a guest at a tea party, he seemed, in the course of this, to have entered into a dispute with a lady painter (caused by his saying that no woman could be a great painter, since she could not have the physical stamina to walk fifty miles a day, which, he said, was necessary to a painter, owing to the constant withdrawing from, and then advancing towards, the canvas).

Not having heard her name, he asked me to make enquiries as to her identity, and described her aspect thus: "Large washed face, yellow fox fur, old Scotch gentleman, ver' old, ver' obstinate."

After he had left Paris for the United States, just before the second war, he wrote to me once a week. (He became, eventually, an American citizen.)

After the outbreak of war, one letter he wrote to me caused a certain flutter in the censorship. This was while he was still learning to speak English, which he did, in the end, flawlessly.

"This month," he wrote, "all my conversations are

with Katz." (He shared my affection for cats.) "But my
beloved, he leave me again! Always two times each year,
he leave me to get married. But he come back, you see!
What you think of English now? Going well? Badly?
You tell me."

When at last, after a month or so, the letter reached
me, it was striped like Blake's Tiger with many hues,
having been examined for invisible ink. For was it not
obvious that Katz must be the name of a very low spy?
Was the letter not written, also, in some kind of code,
and, finally, did not the enquiry "What you think of
English now?" refer to the advance or otherwise of our
armies, not to his progress in our language?

He died, in Rome, in the summer of 1957. But his
power of living was so great that I cannot believe I shall
never see him again.

Thinking of him now, I see him as I saw him shortly
after our first meeting. The snow was thick on the
ground, and he was leaping in the air and clapping his
large painter's hands together, because the snow reminded him of his childhood and youth, before the
misery and grandeur began.

CHAPTER SEVENTEEN

I Am About to "Scrutinise"
A Bouquet of Flowers for the Critics

It may be said that the arts are life accelerated and concentrated. They are the voice of the sibyl, telling us of the secret that is behind life.

The violence of an epoch is responsible for the technical experiments of painters and poets of today. How to attain speed is the problem. And, as far as poets are concerned, to do this we must study the effect of texture on rhythm. These experiments are, for the most part, of a violent order. And if you ask why rhythms have become more violent, the answer is: this is an age of machinery, a wild race for time, confined within limits that are at once mad and circumscribed. Try to get out, and you will knock your head against the walls of materialism. This state of things is mirrored in modern syncopated dance-music, which removes music from the world of inspiration (which evolves itself organically from the inner need of the artist) and brings it into the world of machinery, where form is superimposed as a logical idea. There is no time or space in which to dream. It is because of this that in those poems which deal with the world crumbling into dust, or with materialism building monstrous shapes out of the deadened dust, I, for one, use the most complicated dance-rhythms which could be found, or else syncopated rhythms which are not dance-rhythms.

With the publication of Mr. T. S. Eliot's first book of poems, *Prufrock*, a new era in poetry began. There was, of course, the usual howl of rage that greets every great work of art when it is new and unaccustomed, mainly because the public has got into the way of thinking that man has always seen as he sees now. This is wrong. Not only has he seen with different eyes, but it is impossible that we should all see alike at the present time, although the crowd would prefer uniformity of sight. The modernist artist gives us the chance of exerting our individuality in seeing. The older beauty, the beauty of the old masters, is the beauty of species and mass—the new beauty is highly individualised and separate. The modern artist is not concerned with things in the mass, he is passionately interested in the fulfilling of the destinies of the single individuals that make up the mass—whether these individuals are men, or leaves, or waves of the sea. The great quality of the old masters is force, used in the scientific term of the word—the binding together of the molecules of the world. That is partly what makes their sense of design so tremendous. The great quality of the modern masters is an explosive energy, the separating up of the molecules, exploring the possibilities of the atom.

This is at once the quality and the danger of pioneer poetry. The aim of the modernist poets—the constant aim—is to reconcile this necessity of exploring the possibilities of the atom with the necessity for logical design and form. The primary needs in poetry today are a greater expressiveness, a greater formality, and a return of rhetoric (good rhetoric, be it understood). Expressiveness and rhetoric mean almost, but not quite, the same thing. Bad rhetoric, by which I mean superimposed rhetoric—images which are meaningless and unrelated to the material and shape of the poem—is bad poetry. It was bad poetry which produced Stephen Phillips. But with the exception of Wordsworth, all our greatest poetry has been created, partly, by its rhetoric. Examine Milton for the truth of this. We must fear the debilitated state and lowered vitality which is shown by the outcry for understatement, for quietness, for neutral tints in poetry.

These words were written while I was living in Paris, and I quote them here for obvious reasons.

I cannot claim that this chapter, which I have subtitled "A Bouquet of Flowers for the Critics," comes in chronological order. But "as it was in the beginning. . . ." Anybody who knows me will agree that, without it, no book of mine would be complete.

"No individual must think himself more brilliant than his fellows. We must have no intellectuals. Each mind is of equal importance"—Bernhardt Rust, Reichminister of Culture and Education, quoted in *Our Time*, January, 1946.

Dr. F. R. Leavis, however, whom I am about to "scrutinise," is an Intellectual.

Stranger: "I do seem to see one very large and bad sort of ignorance which . . . may be weighed in the scale against all other sorts of ignorance put together."

Theatetus: "What is it?"

Stranger: "When a person supposes that he knows, and does not know; this appears to be the great source of all the errors of the intellect."

Theatetus: "True."

Stranger: "And this, if I am not mistaken, is the kind of ignorance which especially earns the title of stupidity."

Theatetus: "True."

It is both instructive and pleasurable to study the works of those living critics whose ears, long as they may be, seem not to have been constructed for the hearing of poetry.

Dr. F. R. Leavis's pronouncements are a constant pleasure to one. For one thing, he has a transcendental gift, even when he is writing sense, of making it appear to be nonsense. With this, he has a genuine, natural, and cultivated gift for wincing—which, from time to time, makes him resemble a ruthless, yet graciously antiseptic young dentist discovering the root of the trouble and explaining it to the patient.

He is frank and he is fearless. Writing of Tiresias in Mr. T. S. Eliot's *Waste Land*, after commenting: "The

170

two sexes meet in Tiresias . . ." he informs us that a cultivated modern is, or feels himself to be, intimately aware of the experience of the opposite sex.

When Dr. Leavis writes of Mr. D. H. Lawrence, he seems to combine the fervour of a dear old country clergyman preaching a sermon on the Woman Taken in Adultery, with the powers of expression of those interesting persons who are placed in charge of a Sultan's harem.

But happiest of all is the moment when we read Dr. Leavis on the subject of Milton, whom he decided to show up in his magazine *Scrutiny*. He has decided that there is very little of interest to be found in Milton. The sound of a great deal of Milton's poetry, too, affects Dr. Leavis much as the sound of a motor bicycle affects my less sensitive nervous system. "We find ourselves . . . flinching from the foreseen thud that comes so inevitably, and, at last, irresistibly; for reading *Paradise Lost* is a matter of resisting, of standing up against the verse-movement, or subduing it into something tolerably like sensitiveness, and in the end our resistance is worn down, we surrender at last to the inexplicable monotony of the ritual."

This thunderbolt is followed by a lot of the usual wincing and whimpering about "sensitiveness" and by an analysis of the following passage:

> *The hasty multitude*
> *Ad*miring *enter'd, and the work some praise*
> *And some the Architect: his hand was known*
> *In Heav'n by many a Towred structure high,*

171

Where Scéptr'd Angels held their résidence,
And sat *as Princes . . .*

It is sad to see Milton's great lines bobbing up and down in the sandy desert of Dr. Leavis's mind with the grace of a fleet of weary camels.

Recently, a person named D. J. Enright (whoever he may be), tiring of washing his knickerbockers in the Pierian springs and playing yo-yo with his Adam's apple on the lowest slopes of Mount Parnassus, wrote to the *New Statesman:* "Writers who detach tragedy from the persons who suffer it are generally to be seen soon after wearing someone else's bleeding heart on their own safe sleeves—an odious transaction, and an odious transaction is what Dame Edith Sitwell's atomic poetry seems to me to be."

It would not enter my head to wonder in what light Mr. Enright regarded my poetry. But here are three lines from one of my odious transactions, "Dirge for the New Sunrise: Fifteen minutes past eight o'clock, on the morning of Monday the 6th of August, 1945."

Bound to my heart as Ixion to the wheel,
Nailed to my heart as the Thief upon the Cross,
I hang between our Christ and the gap where
the world was lost.

And here are four lines of the tuneless gibberish (the sound is really appalling) written by this person, presumably partly about a love affair and partly about nuclear warfare—if it is about anything at all. The incompetence is such that nothing is clear, excepting that he is grumbling, in a weak manner, about something.

> *Someone else has stepped in there,*
> *While you were—where?—were elsewhere:*
> *Well-chosen words to sway against or for,*
> *Conventional and nuclear, peace and war.*

One word seems to him as another, and I suppose he picked up the word "nuclear" somewhere or other.

And here is a verse from another alleged poem of his which he has had the impudence to call "A Fine and Private Place" (the poem from which he snitched that phrase was the work of a great poet).

> *It was fine, it was private, it was busy.*
> *There he was, with his fingers crossed,*
> *And a dead hand hung against the lively eye,*
> *Doing what was expected of him,*
> > *twenty-four hours a day,*
> *Feeding the worms out of his flesh,*
> *As was right, as was proper,*
> *Enriching his piece of earth.*

Mr. Enright is not, I believe, more dead than usual. I do not understand, therefore, his remark about "writers who detach tragedy from the persons who suffer it."

Another poet of an equal eminence produced, some years ago, this line:

> *Deliver us from fornication and hockey.*

* * *

From Mr. Robert Conquest's preface to the anthology *New Lines:* " . . . the restoration of a sound and fruitful attitude to poetry, of the principle that poetry is written by and for the whole man, intellect, emotions, senses and all."

Two lines from Mr. Conquest's "Humanities," an alleged poem appearing in the anthology for which he makes the above claim:

> *Is it, when paper roses make us sneeze,*
> *A mental or a physical event?*

I live so far from le beau monde that I have no paper roses, so cannot answer that question, of world-shaking importance though it be, and written, as it is, "for the whole man, intellect, emotions, senses and all."

Mr. Conquest again, in a review of Roy Fuller in *The Spectator*, January, 1958: "He finds a more powerful and vivid material in minor events and appearances than the Cain-and-crucifixion lot can in all their galaxies of blood and fire. Perhaps his more sublunar images do just occasionally make for a certain amount of dead weight—the life of a lung-worm is just a trifle undramatic when it comes to sustaining a forty-two line allegory."

Surely not!

Note: I am the only poet who writes of Cain and of the Crucifixion, because, although I have neither resources of language, intellect, sense, nor feeling, I regard these as slightly more important themes than sneezing at paper roses, or the life of a lung-worm.

174

Mr. Fuller wrote a poem about finding a spider in his bath.

The Times Literary Supplement, August, 1954: "One difficulty, of course, which a modern critic finds in dealing with such a poet . . . is that his attention is concentrated on words. For (X) . . . words in themselves have always been a matter of secondary importance. (X) is not a poet of brilliant sudden comprehensions, of striking individual lines or passages, and she does not bother at all about whether the words that are adequate to her thoughts may evoke in readers of another temperament irrelevant stock responses. . . . The frailty of the poems is their distinction. At their very best, they seem to be just on the verge of being not there at all."

"The mind," I remember Miss —— (the poet in question) saying to me, "is a vortex."

Note: "Mind and matter," said the lady with the wig, "glide swift into the vortex of immensity. Howls the sublime, and softly sleeps the calm ideal in the whispering chambers of Imagination. To hear it, sweet it is. But then, out laughs the stern philosopher, and saith to the Grotesque 'What ho! Arrest for me that agency. Go, bring it here!' And so the vision fadeth."

Times Literary Supplement, November, 1957 (the following was written admiringly): "One is reminded of the great actress whose advice to aspirants was to think of next week's laundry-list in the middle of a love-scene."

The Spectator—AT IT AGAIN: Mr. Kingsley Amis in that paper, November, 1957 (a review of Sir Sidney Colvin's *Keats* speaks of " . . . that sugary erotic extravaganza 'The Eve of St. Agnes' "): "Even in his best poems Keats devotes himself too uncritically to 'the world of the imagination.' Even 'The Ode to the Nightingale,' though containing passages which must delight the most jaded, is full of frigidities, of appeals to the remote and merely fanciful."

Years ago, criticism consisted of a noisy bumptiousness. This was superseded by a terrified crawling, of the kind described by Sir James Frazer, in a passage translated from *Histoire de la Nouvelle France:* "A North American Indian is known to have fondled a dead mouse, in order to appease the genius of mice."

This is the attitude adopted by certain critics towards the unhappy little people who, by means of an incessant squealing, are hoping to attain fame.

Were I not too kind to laugh at the cruel disappointment and envy suffered by certain poor little unsuccessful writers, I might be amused by the fact that although I am now seventy-seven years of age, the unsuccessful are still thrown into what is practically an epileptic fit brought on by envy and malice at the mere mention of my name.

I understand that persons of that kind think I am laughing at them.

On the contrary, I think it is very clever of them to discover each other—although when they do so it must give them the feeling we experience when coming face to face with our own image in a mirror—they are all exactly alike. Still they can admire each other, mirrored, and that must be a great comfort to them. I have nothing against them as writers excepting for three things:

   I. *They have not an idea of any importance.*
  II. *They do not know one word from another.*
 III. *They can't write.*

I understand that they aim at purity and clarity, with the result that each of their poems resembles a glass of tepid lemonade in which a couple of teaspoonfuls of Matthew Arnold have been dissolved.

CHAPTER EIGHTEEN

A World of Shadow

E very day, unless the grey prison bars of the rain
were so thick that we must remain indoors, we
sat in the porch of Renishaw, on the north side of
the dark and shadowed house. There was nothing to
look at, excepting the far brightness of two cornfields,
and some magnificent trees, whose shadow seemed always to be upon our house. Indeed, we were like people
who walk for ever under the shadow of immemorial
trees.

But on the south side are the large and sunny gardens,
warmth and clouds of odour and of colour, and bees so
like the warm and buzzing lights, bee-winged light so
like the honey-makers, that one could hardly know one
from the other. The enormous elms of the avenue shed
now their green and golden dust, the fantasies splash,
the eternal statues have forgotten everything that was
mournful in their past.

On the south side of Renishaw were the huge and
dreamlike gardens, haunted, the flowers were some-

times shy as the dreams of youth, or they were laughing, with all the wisdom of maturity.

Why did we find ourselves walking in a tomb full of dead and frozen things? We who were young, bathed in the airs of beauty that came from an undying and youthful sea, should have been flying across the grass while the dews from some brighter heaven than we know fall upon our hair, or listening to music, that vast and inevitable structure. I think that nothing is more melancholy than the dying fall of music heard beside some waterfall—where the statues, left from some greater civilisation, remind us of the beauty which is no longer with us, which has been buried for a while beneath the earth.

But ours was a world of shadow, and of unmistakable shadows, although the passing sound of that far-off music among the ruins was for ever with us.

The second world war came and went. I had managed to leave Paris and return to England before hostilities began and was one of the millions who suffered the minor restrictions and the major terrors of this time. I began to receive invitations to give poetry recitals, sometimes alone, sometimes with my brother Osbert, sometimes with Dylan Thomas, and can remember at least one occasion when, reciting to a group of servicemen, I heard the familiar, heart-stopping whine of a doodle-bug. Perhaps everybody in that room wondered whether we should throw ourselves under tables or just run for our lives. I went on reading and the bomb passed overhead.

After a year of war I began to write poetry again—I

had written nothing after *Gold Coast Customs*—of the
state of the world, of the terrible rain

> *Dark as the world of man, black as our loss—*
> *Blind as the nineteen hundred and forty nails*
> *Upon the Cross—*

falling alike upon guilty and guiltless, upon Dives
and Lazarus, until

> *Under the Rain the sore and the gold are as one.*

I wrote of the sufferings of Christ, the Starved Man
hung upon the Cross, the God of the Poor Man, who
bears in His Heart all wounds.

In one poem I wrote of the world reduced to the Ape
as mother, teacher, protector.

But, too, with poor Christopher Smart, I blessed
Jesus Christ with the Rose and his people, which is a
nation of living sweetness.

My time of experiments was done.

Before the time came for "The Shadow of Cain" to be
written, various of my poems spoke of the change from
the worship of the holy, living, life-giving gold of the
wheat to the destructive gold of Dives—the change from
the warmth of love that makes all men brothers to the
state in which men only call their fellow-men "Brother"
in order to act the part of Cain.

In "The Two Loves," a poem written about eighteen
months before "The Shadow of Cain," I wrote of the
summer of the earth and of the heart, when

> *. . . In such a heat of the earth, under*
> *The red bough, the Colossus of rubies the first*

180

> *husbandman and gravedigger, the red Adam,*
> *Dug from the earth of his own nature the corn effigy*
> *Of a long-buried country god, encrusted with*
>   *earth-virtues. . . .*

Then the warmth of the heart had gone, only a false brotherhood remained. But still the sun itself had not been harnessed into a war-machine against us.

> *Gone is that heat. But this is the hour of brother-*
>   *hood, the warmth that comes*
> *To the rejected by Life—the shadow with no eyes—*
> *Young Icarus with the broken alar bones*
> *And the sapped and ageing Atlas of the slums*
> *Devoured by the days until all days are done—*
> *To the Croesus of the breadline, gold from the*
>   *sun. . . .*

In "The Shadow of Cain," however, we moved still further from the Sun that is Christ and the Sun of the heart. The poem is about the fission of the world into warring particles, destroying and self-destructive. It is about the gradual migration of mankind, after that Second Fall of Man that took the form of the separation of brother and brother, of Cain and Abel, of nation and nation, of the rich and the poor—the spiritual migration of these into the desert of the Cold, towards the final disaster, the first symbol of which fell on Hiroshima.

The poem came into being thus.

On the 10th of September, 1945, my brother Osbert and I were in the train going to Brighton, where we were to give a reading. He pointed out to me a para-

graph in *The Times*, a description by an eye-witness of
the immediate effect of the atomic bomb upon Hiroshima. That witness saw a totem pole of dust arise to
the sun as a witness against the murder of mankind. . . . A totem pole, the symbol of creation, the
symbol of generation.

From that moment the poem began, although it was
not actually written until April of the next year. It
passed through many stages.

I wrote how, after the desert of the Cold, the wander-
ers reached an open door, although all that was left to
them were the primal Realities.

> *And when we reached an open door*
> *The Fate said, "My feet ache."*
> *The Wanderers said, "Our hearts ache."*
>
> *There was great lightning*
> *In flashes coming to us over the floor:*
> *The Whiteness of the Bread*
> *The Whiteness of the Dead*
> *The Whiteness of the Claw*
> *All this coming to us in flashes through*
>   *the open door.*

I dreamed those lines, about two months before I began
to write the poem as a whole. The open door, in my
dream, was the door of birth—through which we would
come to Bread, Struggle (the Claw), and Death. As I
used the symbol of the door in the poem, it is still the
door of birth; but it is also the door through which we
must find our own path. The three lightnings are still
those three primal Realities. Reduced to these, in the

very house of Birth and of Death, having found our way
in the desert of the Cold, I saw the Spring returning.
There was still the grandeur of the Sun, and of Christ
returning to us with the life-giving wheat of harvest.

And everywhere
The great voice of the Sun in sap and bud
Fed from the heart of Being, the panic Power,
The sacred Fury, shouts of Eternity,
To the blind eyes, the heat in the wingèd seed, the
  fire in the blood. . . .

But then came the horror, the symbol of which was
seen by that witness at Hiroshima:

We did not heed the Cloud in the Heavens shaped like
  the hand
Of Man . . .
      . . . the Primal Matter
Was broken, the womb from which all life began.
Then to the murdered Sun a totem pole of dust arose
  in memory of Man.

CHAPTER NINETEEN

Vulgarity as It Has Been, Will Be, Ever Shall Be, Amen

People are constantly asking me what I think of—
for instance—Angry Young Men. On this and
other subjects I prefer to be silent, except to say that
they are not angry enough. Compare their peevish outbursts with the anger of Swift, or of my brother
Sacheverell in his book *Splendours and Miseries*, and
you will see what I mean. But, in choosing to write a
book about the past, I have spared myself the need to
express my views on the present. Perhaps this is just as
well! I did, however, come across some thoughts I put
together on the subject of vulgarity. It seems to me that
these apply as much now as when I wrote them, and so I
have decided to include them.

* * *

A short time ago, when writing about *The Dunciad*, a poem which is, to my mind, one of the greatest in the English language, I reflected that Vulgarity is, in reality, nothing but a modern, chic, pert descendant of the goddess Dullness. Should we penetrate into the home of Vulgarity, we should find—repainted, no doubt, or else hung in an inconspicuous corner—the old Family Portrait of Dullness, and the face would show the very features of her great descendant; the same simper, the same vacuity. One difference, however, would lie in the fact that the lady in the portrait wears a dress of modest cut and material, whilst her great-granddaughter shows as much of herself as possible—the rest being covered with shiny oil-cloth. The other difference is that whilst Dullness does not treat Respectability as an outcast, Respectability is, actually, the only outcast with whom Vulgarity is not on speaking terms.

When writing a biography it is always best to trace the life of the object of our veneration from its beginning. We must not show our hero or heroine midway in his or her career, entering into society, or making a mark upon the world. We must be present at the birth, listen to the cradle-songs, admire the first prattlings, witness the education. But should we attempt the task of writing the life-history of the goddess who, with her brother Mammon, rules the modern world, we should find various difficulties in the way. The date of our heroine's birth is, for instance, unknown. She seems as old as the world; she must, we think, have been with us always; yet, actually, although the conduct of King Charles the Second and His Majesty Louis the

Fifteenth, the amour of Lord Nelson with Lady Hamilton, presage not only her birth but her maturity, we shall find no hint of the goddess's presence in literature (either English or continental) until the middle of the nineteenth century. It cannot be said that Vulgarity was a companion of Monsieur Jourdain, for instance, nor of the Précieuses Ridicules, nor of Mrs. Malaprop, since pretensions that are quite innocent and that harm no one can scarcely be said to be vulgar; they are often the result of one form of starvation, are, at the worst, only an excuse for a gentle laughter on the part of the spectator.

Nor, again, is Vulgarity to be found in the novels of Smollett, or in the works of Rabelais or Swift, since coarseness on great lines and impelled by serious motives does not constitute Vulgarity; coarseness, however, cannot afford to be a dwarf or to snigger—and I wish certain modern dramatists could remember this.

Vulgarity is never free—is invariably trammelled by conventions (bottle and pyjama parties, for instance, are bound up with the idea that to be decent is to be a prig). Vulgarity is never healthy. Is Falstaff vulgar? Was Marie Lloyd vulgar?

Although the birth-date of the great goddess is unknown, it may, or may not, have occurred somewhere in the middle or towards the end of the nineteenth century, and supporting this conjecture we find at about this time a perfect shower of memoirs of Courtesans, a general worship of this genus of being. It was then, for instance, that Grand Dukes adopted as an industry the habit of drinking champagne out of the shoes of these young persons—to my mind, an insanitary custom, and one lacking in what the advertisements would call "personal freshness"—and it was at about this time that Monsieur Dumas produced his nonsense about *La Dame aux Camélias*. If, however, we believe the goddess to be younger than the heroine of Monsieur Dumas's play, then I, for one, should imagine—at a rough guess—that she was born in the Edwardian era, and for birthplace give her America, or perhaps England—but I am inclined to think America.

Even in the cradle the goddess took to herself emblems and signs: court painters, attitudes and points of view, flowers which she made particularly her own, such as the Rambler Rose (the Queen of this species being that known as "Dorothy Perkins"), and, above all, the creed that a lack of heart constitutes a sign of good sense and of good breeding. Hearts were, however, encouraged if they were likely to lead to the Divorce Court; and the goddess invented a new type of heroine, one who threw her heart about as if it were a nice hard tennis-ball. She invented the Woman with the Past.

It was not, however, until after the first world war that Vulgarity came into her own, with the hordes of newly enriched or semi-rich "fashionable" people who now infest our land or perform rat-like excursions in hordes to the Lido. Gone, thank heavens, are the bottle and pyjama parties of ten years ago, the "original" parties, the parties given to celebrate a divorce. Gone, too, are the lesser bores and horrors: the skirts worn above the knees, the Eton crop, the platinum blondes, the treasure-hunts. Yet still discreet and ageless women, the ghosts of fashionable restaurants, waiting, watching, pondering and pandering, discover, chronicle, and hymn the praises of the newest fashions in behaviour, customs, and persons—of the fashion of having no face, for instance (for faces, my children, have gone completely out of fashion, they are no longer worn). They discover the fashion of "fork luncheons," to be eaten standing up by busy women with nothing whatever to do—women who are too busy to do more than walk into the dining-room of their hostess and gulp down her food and drink. They discover new "interesting personalities," and each of these indomitable climbers strongly resembles

> . . . *bold Arnall; with a weight of skull*
> *Furious he dives, precipitately dull.* . . .
> *No crab more active in the dirty dance,*
> *Downward to climb, and backward to advance,*
> *He brings up half the bottom on his head,*
> *And loudly claims the Journals and the Lead.*

The waiting, watching chroniclers discover as well new words for the enhancement of our smartness: "shy-making" and "bogus" a few years ago, and now "eats"—a particularly trying substitute for wit. And, oh, the new smart voices that echo these! If feminine, these voices are either deliberately colourless and wooden, rich and artificially hoarse, or tinny and tiny and as circumscribed and meaningless as if they issued from an inferior and worn-out musical box. If masculine, they are as high and piercing and meaningless as the shriek of a parrot or a peacock. If feminine, they echo not only

188

the new fashionable catchword, but also gros mots and bad language. If masculine, they screech "darlings" and "too heavenlies" and the latest news from the Paris dressmakers' establishments. Looking at these young gentlemen (who are, if possible, even worse than the women), we are reminded once again of *The Dunciad*, this time of the image formed by the hands of "gentle Dulness":

> *All as a partridge plump, full fed and fair,*
> *She form'd this image of well-bodied air;*
> *With pert flat eyes she window'd well its head,*
> *A brain of Feathers, and a heart of Lead; . . .*
> *Never was dash'd out, at one lucky hit,*
> *A Fool so just a copy of a Wit. . . .*

They are, however, ashamed of their creator, and the voices which are their outposts are believed by them to be a fortification or protection against her.

These young men (the women are, for the most part, simply faceless ninnies following the lead of the young men) may, indeed, be said to be acolytes and pages of the newer Vulgarity, with their screams about "chic" and their adolescent cravings for the all-new both in house-decoration and in clothes—drawing-room walls covered in boot-buttons, pearl buttons, or straw, furniture made of steel, oil-cloth dresses for the faceless, international amateur film-stars of the Lido, Paris, and London. Yes, I think it may be said with truth that the young men are even more fervent worshippers of the goddess than the young women; they are more terrified to be a fortnight behind the latest fashions; the name of the latest book or piece of music is often upon their lips. For, worst of all, they have taken up and are explaining the arts as a means to social climbing. The only way in which we can prove a love of the arts is by helping the artist, when possible; these people do nothing but waste the artist's time—they extend no helping hand.

And, speaking of the arts, we must remark that in these a new form of Vulgarity reigns. In the case of Vulgarity's court painters in the Edwardian era, it was thought necessary that a heavy air of repletion should brood over all the froth—the chiffon scarves, the feathers, the curtains; I mean repletion on the part of the painter. A feeling was conveyed that even if the sitter was represented standing against the pillars of a terrace, or under an ancient tree, the portrait was actually *painted* in the dining-room; whilst portions of the sitter's anatomy or clothing must, if possible, resemble some article of food. Thus, ladies' hands frequently presented a strong likeness to slices of boneless smoked salmon; their dresses were often compounded of whipped cream.

So much for the Past! But now all is changed as regards the pictorial art: and emptiness has become a necessity. In literature, however, quite a new form of Vulgarity reigns supreme; and certain lady novelists form a corner in it with their determination to face facts, their loud cries of "Use moral Sanitas and Lifebuoy Soap," their noble, healthy-minded "frankness," their political gas-works, their "bravery," their open-mindedness, their insistence that we should inspect the emotional sanitary systems of their characters, and their

190

habit of praising any book produced by a member of their own order which talks nonsense about women being superior to men or to "women's work." They behave as if woman was a rabbit and had suddenly learnt to use her paws.

This is the heavier type of Vulgarity; the frothier, Lido-haunting, "smart" type would, I imagine, laugh at the Vulgarity to which gentility bows the knee. Yet in reality they are sisters. Both kinds have an abject fear of other people's opinions; neither are free. It is no less vulgar to be afraid, if we are "chic," that this or that Leader of Society may think we ought to have our walls covered with boot-buttons instead of straw than it is to be afraid, if we live in the suburbs, that Mrs. Jones will think we use the wrong kind of cocoa, or will notice the washing hanging on the clothes-line. Why can we not do as we like?

To sum up: Vulgarity is often, in a sense, nothing but Fear in disguise, a fear that affects the rich. For Vulgarity is not a quality of the very poor. There is nothing vulgar about the crowds on a Bank Holiday riding donkeys on the sands, or whirling about in a merry-go-round, shrimping, paddling, or eating winkles. Vulgarity has never yet worn a simple dress.

CHAPTER TWENTY

Roy Campbell and Dylan Thomas

Before the last war was ended I met almost everybody whom I now regard as my friends.

Two young men—they were still young when they died—who were my friends and were both great poets were Roy Campbell and Dylan Thomas.

Roy Campbell was one of the very few great poets of our time. His poems are of a great stature, and have a giant's strength and power of movement. They have, too, an extraordinary sensuous beauty. Everything is transformed to greatness—as when, in that superb poem "The Vision of Our Lady over Toledo," he describes the jasmine clinging like "thunder to the peaks" or making a "dewy starlight with its shade."

Sometimes he produced "a fierce animal line," "canalising brute light and heat" (to quote a phrase about certain painting, from Jean Helion's "Avowals and Comments"). Or he rushes with the speed of a whirlwind, and with an equal strength.

Such a rush of wind is to be found in these lines from "Horses on the Camargue":

When hail and fire converge,
The only souls to which they strike no pain
Are the white-crested fillies of the surge
And the white horses of the windy plain.
Then in their strength and pride
The stallions of the wilderness rejoice;
They feel their Master's trident in their side,
And high and shrill they answer to his voice.
With white tails smoking free,
Long streaming manes, and arching necks, they show
Their kinship to their sisters of the sea—
And forward hurl their thunderbolts of snow.
Still out of hardship bred,
Spirits of power and beauty and delight
Have ever on such frugal pastures fed
And loved to course with tempests through the night.

Emerson said of Plato that "he, from the sunlike centrality and reach of his vision, had a faith without cloud." This might have been said of Roy Campbell.

His language had the "ultimate quality" that Ben Jonson said was necessary to poetry, and an extraordinary technique that varied from that of the lines describing the dead Mazeppa to the exquisite, cool, vital, dancing sound of "The Palm"—a sound which seems, actually, to reproduce that of air moving among the leaves. I quote these few lines (he was writing about the sand at the root of the palm):

193

For bitter and cold though it rasp to my root,
Each atom of gold is the chance of a fruit,
The sap is the music, the stem is the flute,
And the leaves are the wings of the seraph I shape
Who dances, who springs in a golden escape,
Out of the dust and the drought of the plain,
To sing with the silver hosannas of rain.

Or take, as a contrast, that great, terrible, and moving poem "To a Pet Cobra," a poem which seems to me to have the same greatness as certain poems of Baudelaire's and which begins:

With breath indrawn and every nerve alert,
As at the brink of some profound abyss,
I love on my bare arm, capricious flirt,
To feel the chilly and incisive kiss
Of your lithe tongue that forks its swift caress
Between the folded slumber of your fangs,
And half reveals the nacreous recess
Where death upon those dainty hinges hangs

and again, the water-lapping beauty, the ineffable sound, of the translation from St. John of the Cross, "Upon a Gloomy Night."

But I must speak of him as a human being. Of great stature, build, strength, and vitality, he had eyes of the flashing blue of the kingfisher. One would have noticed him anywhere, towering above the crowd, not only because of his height, and certainly not because of any flaunting characteristics—he was utterly lacking in affectation in appearance or manner—but because of his

194

extraordinary personality.

He had a great simplicity, and his courtesy and sweetness to his friends could not have been greater. Fantastically brave and chivalrous, he had the simple heart and the faith of a child. He would have been more at home in the Tudor age than in this age of the barren grey creeds, of the dictators who could see mankind as "planet bacilli"! He was made of "the wild nature of the world." He has been accused of being, to use Boehme's expression, a fascist. He was never a fascist. But, a deeply religious man, he fought against the Reds in Spain. He believed, as I believe, that it is equally infamous to massacre priests, nuns, Jews, peasants, and aristocrats. He could also never be forgiven because he was passionately loyal to the monarchs of England.

I have never known a more vitalising companion, nor one who had stranger adventures. These were sometimes so extraordinary that people who did not know him well could not, at first, believe they had happened. And yet they invariably had.

Who but he would have had his motor charged (in an African forest) by a rhinoceros who—which was unusual, to say the least of it—won the battle and disappeared into the forest bearing the bonnet of the motor on his horn as a trophy? Who but he would (when, during the last war, he was Sergeant Major of a company of African troops) have been put in charge of an Irish Baronet addicted to the practice of black magic, the knowledge of which fact changed the complexion of the troops from black to pale grey, with orders to lose him as soon as possible? So Roy took him away and lost him. Who but he would, as a child, have turned octopuses inside out when they were threatening trouble?

He enjoyed battles.

When last in Africa (at the time of the rhinoceros trouble), he sent me a postcard depicting a particularly benevolent-looking sleeping lion, and bearing the words "How is *The* —— [mentioning a weekly paper that had been offering me impertinences] behaving? I shall be in Europe again in a few weeks time. *Would you like me to come over?*" I tremble to think of the fate of the staff of that paper if he *had!*

The battle with the rhinoceros was, I think, the only one he ever lost. But there were moments when his chosen adversaries showed a regrettable reluctance to fight. There is a certain University Don who, wincing and whimpering, has denounced almost all of the most vital poets of our time. Roy determined to defy him in his own surroundings. He therefore went to the University in question and gave a lecture to an enormous crowd of undergraduates (most of them delighted, some, under the mousy spell of this semi-Eminence Grise, disapproving) in which he said, in no uncertain terms, what he thought of him. On this being reported to the Don, that gentleman became a little nervous and said he would have to "hire a bodyguard." Whereupon Roy wrote to him these words: "You go ahead and hire a bodyguard. And I'll walk into your College and tear the clothes off your back, and by the time I've done with you, your wife and children won't know you. And I'll walk out of the College without a single scratch on me!" "And do you know, Edith," he said to me, "*the creature*

196

didn't even answer!"

Nietzsche, writing of Petronius, said he had "the feet of a wind, the rush, the breath, the emancipating scorn of a wind, which makes everything healthy, by making everything run."

This might have been said of Roy. But I do not like the word "scorn," and it is not Roy's satires (some of which, to my deep regret, are about people who are my friends) but such poems as "To a Pet Cobra," the magnificent, strong "Horses on the Camargue," the wonderful poem to his beloved wife in the second volume of his *Collected Poems*, and "The Vision of Our Lady over Toledo" in the same volume, that prove him the great poet that he is. He *did* misunderstand some people completely; but this was the result of terrible circumstances, and if he could only have realized that he had misjudged them, I am certain that he would have made the fullest acknowledgment of this.

He has been much abused for his verbal savagery about the Spanish Reds against whom he fought. But the people who abuse him do not know what certain of those Reds had threatened to do to his beloved wife and his two very young daughters (who were living in Spain, in great danger, while he fought) if they could get hold of them! Roy did not appreciate those threats. Some people are most unreasonable!

This simple giant, with "devocioun in his heart," was the true Knight of Our Lady, and if he had to be taken by death, it was suitable that this should have been when he was returning from the celebration of Her Son's Resurrection.

I think, too, that he, who was all energy, all fire, would have hated to die slowly and helplessly, in bed. He died, as he had lived, like a flash of lightning.

Letter to Mr. Dylan Thomas

Dear Mr. Thomas,

Though we have never met, I am unable to resist writing to you to tell you, however inadequately, with what deep admiration and delight I have read your very beautiful poem which begins with the line

A grief ago

and the beautiful and strange poem in this quarter's *Life and Letters*. It is no exaggeration to say that I do not remember when I have been so moved, profoundly so excited, by the work of any poet of the younger generation, or when I have felt such a deep certainty that here is a poet with all the capabilities and potentialities of greatness. I am completely overcome with this certainty and this admiration. Only a young man who is going to be a great poet could have written the lovely, true, and poignant poem in the programme (the first one, also, has a fine quality)—I cannot recover from it. I think I am learning it by heart.—And as for the poem in *Life and Letters*, only a poet with real greatness could have written those extraordinary second and third lines of the passage which begins:

What is the metre of the dictionary?
The size of genesis? The short spark's gender?
Shade without shape? The shape of Pharaoh's
  echo.

Or the wonderful two lines which begin the poem
—or the line

  Death is all metaphors, shape in one history

I have just finished writing about "A grief ago"
for the London *Mercury*.—My friend Mr. Herring
writes me that a new book of yours will be appearing soon. I have already told my agent that I wish
to review it, but I would be most deeply grateful
if you could tell me who is publishing it, and when
it will appear so that I may make certain to have
the delight and honour of writing about it.—I
have a great admiration, too, for many of your 18
poems, but your two latest have excited and delighted me beyond measure.—I must confess that
the first poem I read of yours I did not like, tech-
nically—and felt it my duty to say so though
without mentioning your name, taking the former
only as an example.

I know now, without any possibility of doubt-
ing it, that in you we have a poet from whom real
greatness may be expected.

This is a very inadequate letter. I hope we may
meet one day. There are innumerable questions I
want to ask you. Your work has, I can assure you,
no more true admirer than

                              Yours sincerely,

This letter was written to Dylan Thomas when he was twenty-two years old. It was the beginning of a friendship that lasted until his tragically early death at the age of thirty-nine. Dylan's early life as a poet was not, in spite of his (very few) champions, easy. Following the publication of his second book, a furious attack on him developed in letters addressed to one of the two principal London newspapers. It was my privilege and pride to give the attackers, during two months, more than as good as they gave. The air still seems to reverberate with the wooden sound of numskulls soundly hit.

I have no memory, and keep no diary, and so, though the occasion was supremely important to me, I cannot remember the exact date of our meeting. I had reviewed his second book and had written the above letter; so when he arrived in London he came to see me.

Poetry is, to some degree, the etheric body of the poet (though to some degree only)—so I will try to describe him physically.

The first time I saw him I felt as if Rubens had suddenly taken it into his head to paint a youthful Silenus. He was not tall, but was extremely broad, and gave an impression of extraordinary strength, sturdiness, and superabundant life. (His reddish-amber curls, strong as the curls on the brow of a young bull, his proud, but not despising, bearing, emphasised this.) Mr. Augustus John's portrait of him is beautiful, but gives him a cherubic aspect which, though pleasing, does not convey, to the present writer at least, Dylan's look of archangelic power.

In full face he looked much as William Blake must have looked as a young man. He had full eyes—like those of Blake—giving at first the impression of being unseeing, but seeing all, looking over immeasurable distances.

I have never known anyone more capable of endearing himself to others. And this was not only the result of his great warmth, charm, and touching funniness. I have never known anyone with a more holy and childlike innocence of mind. The exuberance of his strong physique, of his strong physical life, never marred or blurred that. He loved humanity, and had contempt only for the cruel, the unkind (these are not always identical), and the mean. He was most generous in his enthusiasms and most loyal in his friendships. Alas, that some of the people who crowded round him were unworthy of that noble nature. But these I will leave to their shame. For he is dead. And there is nothing to be done.

When still very young, he married Caitlin Macnamara, the beautiful girl who was the love of his short life. Their mutual love was most touching and beautiful to see. Having supper with me after a Poet's Reading in London, he looked across the table at his young wife with her light bright sparkling hair that seemed to hold all the colour of a spring day, her wild-rose cheeks, and dancing blue eyes, and exclaimed to me, "Isn't she beautiful! *Isn't she beautiful!* From the first moment I saw her, she has been the only one. There never has been, there never will be, anyone but her." On another occasion, the last time I saw him before he died, he was going to America, and she was unhappy because he was going so far away. He said to me, "Tell her, when I am gone, how much I love her." And so now, when he has gone very far away, I do. There was never anyone but her.

He had a speaking voice of the utmost magnificence, range, and beauty, and his speaking of poetry was as sublime as was his writing of poetry. The "lions and fires of his flying breath," to use a phrase of his own, were such that all pride, all light, walked in the lives that, speaking, he made his own. To hear him read Blake's "The Tyger," to hear him read his own poetry, was a revelation. It was a great pride to me to hear him read my own poetry.

Of course there were moments. . . . On one occasion at a tea party given jointly by Carson McCullers and David Gascoyne, Dylan walked over to me and said, sternly, "I hear somebody has been telling you I've been making a beast of myself in Bermondsey. I have *not* been making a beast of myself in Bermondsey."

On another occasion he came to luncheon with me, and, as he arrived, said to me, "I am sorry to smell so awful, Edith. It's Margate." I said, "Yes, of course, my dear boy, it's Margate."

Then there was the occasion, early in our acquaintance, when circumstances prevented him from coming to see me. He wrote one letter of apology which I have lost. Dylan, evidently, was not satisfied with it, and I include his second letter:

> *Cwmdonkin Drive*
> *Uplands*
> *Swansea*

2nd September, 1936
Dear Miss Sitwell,

I know I couldn't have expected you to answer my letter of so many months ago. I was dreadfully rude, not turning up and everything, and I do understand about your not answering my silly letter of apology. But I hope you aren't cross with me really, and I really do want you to believe that I regret—as much as anything in the world—not having continued the friendship I think we began.

Will you meet me again, in spite of things? You're still a great encouragement to me—and always will be—and I do appreciate it.

> *Yours very sincerely,*
> *Dylan Thomas*

In America he was outrageously pursued by a Comus-rout of boring little floozies. I suppose he enjoyed flattery. He did sometimes, I think, have a feeling of bewilderment, and might have said, as Rimbaud said in *Une Saison en Enfer:* "Oui, j'ai les yeux fermés à votre lumière. Je suis une bête, un nègre. Mais je puis être sauvé. Vous êtes de faux nègres, vous, maniaques, féroces, avares. Marchand, tu es nègre; magistrat, tu es nègre; général, tu es nègre; empereux, vielle démangeaison, tu es nègre; tu as bu d'une liqueur non taxée, de la fabrique de Satan." It is hardly necessary to add that the word *nègre* has no reference to the pigmentation of the skin, but is only a word for beings who have never been touched by civilisation.

Dylan has been accused of obscurity. He was, at times, difficult—nobody would deny that. This is partly because of the startling freshness of his images. As Mr. John Crowe Ransom said, "The image cannot be dispossessed of a primordial freshness, which ideas can never claim. An idea is derivative and tamed. The image is in the natural or wild state."

Yet in "Fern Hill" the phrase "happy as the grass was green" must surely be understandable by everybody and has been experienced by everyone. So, too, it must be with this wonderful verse in the same poem:

And then to awake, and the farm, like a wanderer white
With the dew, come back, the cock on his shoulder: it was all
   Shining, it was Adam and maiden,
      The sky gathered again
      And the sun grew round that very day.
So it must have been after the birth of the simple light
In the first, spinning place, the spellbound horses walking warm
      Out of the whinnying green stable
      On to the fields of praise.

He uses, at times, words that seem strange to us. Dr. Marianne Moore quotes the late Wallace Stevens as saying, "Delight lies in flawed words and stubborn sounds." "Or," she continues, "as the metaphorical ox apis might say, 'bull words, aphories.'" Thomas was much addicted to bull words.

Dante, in *De Vulgare Eloquio*, says, "Some words are childish, some womanish, some manly; and of the latter class, some are rustic [sylvan], some urban, and of those which we call urban, we feel some to be combed and slippery, some shaggy and rumpled. Of these, the combed and the rumpled are those which we call grand; but the slippery and the rumpled are those which sound superfluously."

Thomas is, for the most part, "shaggy." The work of Ben Jonson and Donne is often—but not always—"sylvan." Those of Milton and Shelley are "combed." Most of the lesser Augustans must be described as slippery. They seem to have gone to the wrong hairdresser.

I think it was Whitman who said that "even in religious fervor there is always a touch of animal heat." Both religious fervour and animal heat were in his poetry, to the highest degree. His poetry was the "pure fire compressed into holy forms" of which one of Porphyry's Oracles spoke. The generation of those poems was attended by "the great heat" that Aristotle said "attended the generation of lions." To him, blood was spirit.

His was a language "fanned by the breath of Nature, which leaps overhead, cares mostly for impetus and effects, and for what it plants and invigorates to grow" (Whitman: *Notebooks*). He strips from words their old, used, dulling sleepiness and gives them a refreshed and awakened meaning, a new percussion.

As I said in my review of his *Collected Poems*, in the

New York *Herald Tribune*, his voice resembles no other voice; the spirit is that of the beginning of created things; there is here no case of a separate imagination, of invention. From the depths of Being, from the roots of the world, a voice speaks. He might have been, indeed no doubt was, actually writing himself in the lines

> *I, in a wind on fire, from green Adam's cradle,*
> *No man more magical. . . .*

To him, as to Boehme, "the sap in the tree denoteth pure Deity." He loved and praised

the force that through the green fuse drives the flower,

and the

> *. . . animals thick as thieves*
> *On God's rough tumbling grounds*
> *(Hail to His beasthood!)*

(Dylan saw the world as a rough tumbling ground, as a ground for joy and the holy wars of the Spirit.)

With him, all is prayer and praise. Poetry to him is prayer. "When we pray," said the Curé d'Ars, "we should open our heart to God, like a fish when it sees the wave coming." "I am so placed and submerged in his great love, that I seem as though in the sea entirely under water, and can on no side touch, see, or feel anything but water." So said Saint Catherine of Genoa. And so might have spoken Dylan Thomas. But then, as I have said many times, the experiences of the saint and of the great poet are related.

In that great poem "A Refusal to Mourn the Death,

206

by Fire, of a Child in London," with its dark, magnificent, proud movement, we see Death in its reality—as a return to the beginning of things, as a robing, a sacred investiture in those who have been our friends since the beginning of Time:

The grains beyond age, the dark veins of her mother.

(Earth, her mother.) Bird, beast, and flower have their part in the making of mankind.

> *And I must enter again the round*
> *Zion of the water bead*
> *And the synagogue of the ear of corn.*

(The water drop is holy, the wheat ear a place of prayer.) The "fathering and all humbling darkness" itself is a begetting force. Even grief, even tears, are a begetting. "The stations of the breath" are the Stations of the Cross.

With what unalterable sadness, now, does one read these lines to his dying father:

> *Do not go gentle into that good night,*
> *Old age should burn and rave at close of day;*
> *Rage, rage against the dying of the light. . . .*
>
> *Wild men who caught and sang the sun in flight,*
> *And learn, too late, they grieved it on its way,*
> *Do not go gentle into that good night.*

Alas, that he who caught and sang the sun in flight, yet was the sun's brother and never grieved it on its way, should have left us with no goodbye, good night. I shall never hear that golden speaking voice, that voice of the lion, the eagle, the dove, the sun, again. But I, too, must not

. . . blaspheme down the stations of the breath . . .

After the first death, there is no other.

CHAPTER TWENTY-ONE

Butterfly Aspects

Many of my dearest friends are American, and I cannot, although I shall not mention them all personally, finish this book of memories without a word about this warm-hearted, hospitable country.

These are butterfly aspects . . . minor remembrances of a land in which I spent the great part of my time in trains or hotel bedrooms, in the course of a lecture tour or poetry recitals.

In 1948 an invitation came to my brother Osbert and me to give joint recitals, and we arrived in New York to make our first stay in what was to be our home there, the St. Regis Hotel.

I remember our lecture agent, a giant of a man, who, on being instructed by the photographer to stand between Osbert and me and look at us both, shook his head and said sadly, "I can look at one or the other, but not at the two of them together. . . ."

He was immensely reassuring. "Don't be afraid," he said, "I'll see that things are kept in order. When Mrs.

Roosevelt went on tour, the 'boys' were lined up at every station with their brass bands. I swooped her off on an early train and tricked the lot of them. . . ."

My first impressions of New York were overwhelming. Everybody appeared to be young. It was not possible to imagine that people so alive could be old. And the immense blocks of houses lit up by different colours at night like jewels was a sight that has lived in my memory like the burnt gold of the Mexican soil and the strange, touching union of beggars outside the massive churches of this neighbour country. . . .

Feeling so alive in New York, it was difficult to sleep. I do remember on one occasion ringing down to the hall porter and suggesting that I might set up camp in Grand Central Station, as the noise could surely not be so bad. They replied with the impeccable manners always shown me by the staff of this hotel. Even the waiter, Larry, whom I remember chiefly because of an amusing incident involving my brother. Osbert had taken a bath and was drying himself in the bedroom when the door burst open and Larry dashed into his room. Not a bit put out by my brother's naked state, he demanded:

"Sir Charles, where is Miss Smith?" . . . looking around him.

After this I was usually referred to as Miss Smith, but in fact Larry had taken my brother for Sir Charles Mendl, and Miss Smith was his secretary. . . .

As I said, I spent a great deal of time in trains, and among my minor remembrances was my first experience of a phenomenon that I believe is called "Muzak."

When in Paris I bought a record especially for my beloved cat called "Baby Don't Be Blue" and sung by the High Hatted Tragedian of Song. The words, as I remember them, were as follows:

> *O baby don't say you're through,*
> *Baby I'm so blue . . .*
> *Baby . . .*

My cat had a passion for this song, and so I had no difficulty in recognising it when I heard the familiar strains apparently emerging from the compartment next to mine on the train bearing me across America. This was followed by the first part of Grieg's piano concerto, by the march from *Zampa*, a waltz that was played a great deal at seaside hotels during my childhood, and the Priests' March from *Attila*. After which there was a loud click as though somebody had removed their false teeth, and on again with "Baby Don't Be Blue."

This began, as I remember, at seven in the morning and continued until midnight. Knowing that the woman next door had a child with her that doubtless had to be amused, I bore with this concert for the first day uncomplainingly. But when, punctually at seven next morning, it began again, this was too much. I removed my shoe and hammered with all my force on the dividing wall of our two compartments. Then I sent for the porter. He came in with a look of surprise on his face and went at once to a screen at the rear of my compartment. The concert, it seemed, had been self-inflicted. . . .

At one of our recitals, my brother was asked, "How

can you tell good poetry from bad?"

"In the same way as you can tell fish . . . if it's fresh it's good, if it's stale it's bad, and if you're not certain, try it on the cat."

It was during this lecture that my brother made his much-quoted reply to the person in the audience who complained, "We can't hear."

"Then pay attention and you will," he replied.

At every recital in any country in the world there are always two old women who sit together and complain that they cannot hear. When I was reciting with Dylan Thomas, he used to turn to me before the curtain went up and ask, "Where do you suppose the afflicted pair are this time?"

Less pleasant memories of my tours were of English-women encountered en route. One in particular I shall never forget. It was the day that I heard of Roy Campbell's death, and I had gone to bed early, feeling, naturally, greatly upset. The telephone rang and a voice on the other end said, "We're both English, you and I, we should get together and have a good pow-wow. . . ."

Time has drawn a veil over my reply, but I later enquired of the porter whether my caller, who it transpired was a doctor, was male or female. "Ah," the porter replied, "that is what all of us here want to know."

It was in Boston that I encountered my second English-woman. She stopped me as I was getting into the lift at my hotel.

"Ah, Miss Sitwell," she said, "I was so sorry to have missed your little concert."

As it was a recital that had been packed out months in advance, I was not entirely pleased.

"We all missed you terribly," I said to her.

It was in Chicago, I remember, that there was a particularly strong bluish light that played on, and undoubtedly altered the colour of, my aquamarines, which I wore, as always. A furious voice emerged from the audience. "They can't be emeralds," it said. It was in Chicago, also, that I remember a poor man being carried off with an epileptic fit. This happened after I had recited the sleepwalking scene from Lady Macbeth. Telling this story afterwards to Miss Ethel Barrymore, she looked greatly impressed.

"What a compliment!" she said to me.

I remember Chicago chiefly because of the friends I made there. They were a group of charming and lively young people with a keen sense of fun. One morning I received in my post a letter from an admirer which said:

"Wonderful One. Let no danger keep you from us. We are here in these rooms every Monday from 10 am until 10 pm. Monday to Friday. Our Doctor Rabinowitch will tell you what the stars foretell for your poetry and dearest personality. Come wonderful one . . . our girls only live to hold you in their arms."

My young friends put it in an envelope and posted it off to England. They altered one word. Instead of "poetry" they put "criticism" and sent it to a well-known English critic for whom, as I have already made clear in these pages, I had no very high opinion. . . .

These are memories at random. Minor remembrances, as I have said, of a great continent and truly remarkable people. It was a strange irony when, later, I was invited to stay with my dear friends Jock and Betsy Whitney, then Ambassador and Ambassadress in England, at St. Dunstans, their home in Regent's Park, and I realised that this house in which they had made me so happy with the warmth of their friendship was one in which I had been so miserable as a girl, when it was the London house of my Uncle Francis.

Such is the alchemy of goodness. . . .

Los Angeles was the only city in America in which I lived for any length of time.

CHAPTER TWENTY-TWO

Hollywood

The first time I visited Hollywood, at the suggestion of Mr. George Cukor (who had, at one time, the idea that my book *Fanfare for Elizabeth* might be converted into a film), I learned from the newspapers that a little old lady in an ankle-length fur coat and black sandals had crept into Hollywood.

This dwarfish ancient, whose height is five feet eleven, who has never in her life worn black sandals, and who had definitely never *crept anywhere*, was mildly surprised.

As Osbert and I drove the immense distance from the station to the Bel Air Hotel, where we stayed for the first week, the air of early morning seemed full of glamour. Even the streets gave one a feeling of excitement.

The distances in Hollywood and Los Angeles are enormous. Frequently, if asked out to dinner, when one enquired how long it would take to reach the house of one's host, one would be told "Oh, it is quite close. Not more than three quarters of an hour away!"

On our way from the station, we drove between long lines of gigantic palms in the wide boulevards. We passed luxurious houses—the homes of the film stars. Much of Hollywood reminded me strongly of various passages in Arthur Rimbaud's *Les Illuminations*— visions in "Metropolitain," for instance: "Des routes bordées de grilles et de murs, contenant à peine leurs bosquets, et les atroces fleurs qu'on appelerait coeurs et soeurs, Damas damnant de langueur—possessions de féeriques aristocraties ultra-Rhénanes, Japonaises, Guaranies. . . ."

Great golden stars of dew were falling from the tall mimosa-trees, the oleanders, the giant tree-ferns, and the other tropical vegetation. (Although the month was January, the heat was almost tropical.)

People who know nothing of the life in Hollywood have substituted for this a false idea of the lives of artists, engendered, fifty years ago or more, in certain people by Murger's *La Vie de Bohème*. Artists of any worth do not lead lives of that kind, nor do film stars found their lives on such specimens of prose as I am about to parody, and which form the reading matter in the gossip columns of the newspapers.

"Friends of the so-and-sos were falling over each other yesterday, so eager were they to get in first and tell me how they are all shaking their heads over the marriage. It seems that Pixie spat in Bill's face on Saturday at such-and-such a night-club, and he hit her back. They were both thrown out on their ears and continued the fight outside. Pity! They've only been married a fortnight, and though it is only her seventeenth marriage

216

and actually only his fifteenth, friends were afraid they had found happiness at last. And Pixie is such a *lovely* girl and a *perfect little lady!* And Bill, though he ought to be thrown out of the country as a Communist, is just the kind of boy any mother would want her son to be. But now Pixie always stays at home, sulking, and Bill is always about with a beautiful blonde. Pity! Bye-bye till tomorrow. . . .

"Now it seems that Pixie wasn't spitting in Bill's face, she was spitting at Millicent, who is dating Pixie's fourteenth husband, Porky Panzo. Only she missed her. Pity! And Bill didn't hit her. And they weren't turned out of the club. And the beautiful blonde is Bill's sister, Joey. So she isn't a beautiful blonde, though she *is* beautiful and *is* a blonde. And the reason why Pixie never goes out with Bill is because she is going to have a baby (such a little angel—all curls!) at 9:23 next Monday morning. And they have been married for two years, not two weeks. And Bill isn't a Communist. And they are all so happy, and so fond of each other. And Pixie is such a lovely girl, and so is Joey, and Bill is such a lovely boy and—wait till I get my breath back."

In short, "friends" had been at it again.

Only once have I had a frank combat with a lady of this kind. She is serialised in every village *Morticians Do-It-Yourself Home Gazette*, and is by no means an inconsiderable nuisance.

After some months in which she persecuted me weekly ("O.K., Edith, it is only the English language that you are ruining") I wrote and told her that I intended to punish her: "But when I do, you won't know what has hit you! I do not know how to address you. I cannot call you a goose, as geese saved the capitol of Rome, and no amount of cackling on your part would awaken anybody! Nor can I call you an ass, since Balaam's constant companion saw an angel, and recognised it. I can only imagine that you belong to the vegetable tribe, and that all the fizzing and spurting of yours is the result of a vegetable decaying."

There the correspondence ceased. But before this incident I had an encounter with this lady—short, but not nearly short enough.

I was at a party in Hollywood when something or other propelled itself towards me. The man who was talking to me declared that it must be a badly done-up parcel that had been discarded after a Girl Scout encampment, half shielding (though insufficiently) from the public gaze some battered ironmongery and the dear energetic girls' outgoing laundry.

But I am a trained observer, and after a short scrutiny I realised that this object was Miss X, the lady who had been persecuting me for some time. I did not study her face closely, but have been told by one of our most distinguished playwrights that it is a source of some worry to her, since it consists of one "brisk stampede from nose to navel." She wore an extraordinary amount of clothes in some places and—it being the evening—none in others. The same system—if the word may be used in this connection—applied to her hair, which seemed liable to sporadic outbursts in the most unexpected places. It was obvious to the most casual observer that she had her funny little fancies and ways and whims.

As soon as Osbert and I arrived in Hollywood, George Cukor asked us to luncheon. A man of great culture, he is intensely interested, not only in his own art, but in all the arts—and his house, one of the most beautiful in Hollywood, is full of gaiety, charm, and originality. It is quite unlike any other house I know, and reflects in every way its owner's extraordinary subtlety and distinction of mind. Among other treasures he has some exceedingly beautiful eighteenth-century chairs whose backs and seats are made of gigantic mother-of-pearl shells; they have gilded legs. Among his pictures is a particularly lovely Renoir.

He had also—but, alas, no longer—a living treasure in the shape of an enormous black poodle, about the size of a Shetland pony. This dear and lovely creature, Sasha, whose coiffure resembled that of the King of the Cannibal Islands and who was otherwise uncropped, had such a fixation on his master that he would repine, sighing and panting heavily and leaning, in the hope of being comforted, against the bosom of anyone near him, if his master was called away from the room—believing, quite erroneously, that Mr. Cukor had developed the wish to escape from him for ever.

The luncheon party was a large one, and among the guests was Miss Ethel Barrymore, a superb statue endowed with life and with wit, and Miss Merle

Oberon, like a dark and lovely swan.

Next afternoon, one of the gentlemen who was to work with me on the proposed film came to visit me. It was the first time we had met. He is a man with a great sense of fun, but looks very serious. We went over the list of scenes together. "And now we come," said Mr. ——, "to that scene where you have those Cardinal guys threaten the King [Henry the Eighth] with everlasting damnation. And you have the King say to them: 'That's O.K. by me, boys, you go right ahead! And you boys can go tell your boss the Pope that *I am the* King of England. And to *Hell* with his everlasting damnation.'"

Visiting my old friends Aldous and Maria Huxley, I recaptured the fun, the liveliness and happiness of my lost youth.

On one warm afternoon in the garden of their house, Aldous, leaning against the trunk of a tree, began to complain about certain pre-Raphaelite painters: "*Really*, Edith, standing with my back against this tree, I cannot but recollect that picture called *The Long Engagement* in which a curate with long Dundreary whiskers clasps to his heart an etiolated hopeless little woman. On the tree against which he is leaning is cut a heart enclosing their initials."

A hot argument ensued, as to why the engagement had been so long, Aldous holding that this was due to "the great inadequacy of the stipend."

At one party in Hollywood I met Miss Mary Pickford, a confectioner's goddess of vanilla-flavoured ice-cream. She talked to me, at some length, of her role in the part of Little Lord Fauntleroy, and of the serious duty of all artists—that of strengthening the spiritual life of their audience!

I met but few of the stars while I was in Hollywood. In New York I had met Mr. Charles Chaplin and Miss Greta Garbo, the latter a being who is, physically, of the lily tribe, but with a human heart and mind.

But I did meet Miss Marilyn Monroe.

In private life she was not in the least what her calumniators would have wished her to be. She was very quiet, had great natural dignity (I cannot imagine anyone who knew her trying to take a liberty with her), and was extremely intelligent. She was also exceedingly sensitive.

What will-power she must have needed in order to remain the human being she was, after the cruelty with which, in the past, she was treated! That is over now, and she is accepted as the fine artist that she was. But that cruelty was completely odious. It arose partly, I think, from the envy of people who are devoid of beauty, and partly from the heartless stupidity of those who have never known a great and terrifying poverty. There are people, also, who cannot believe that beauty and gaiety are a part of goodness.

When we think of cruelty, we must try to remember the stupidity, the envy, the frustration from which it has arisen. Alexander Pope, in a letter, wrote, "The malice of my calumniators equals their stupidity. I forgive the first, pity the second, and despise both." (Pope himself has been accused of cruelty. But it is a little tiring to be persecuted, unremittingly, for no reason. And perhaps, this being the case with Pope, he thought he would give his persecutors a dose of their own medicine.)

My first meeting with Miss Monroe was when I was living in Sunset Boulevard in an immensely tall house, called Sunset Tower, in which I had a large apartment looked after by Mrs. Pastor, a Hungarian widow, who did my housekeeping. She is like a character created by Shakespeare. I think if one had known Perdita's foster-mother, the Shepherd's wife in *The Winter's Tale*, we should have recognised her as the sister of Mrs. Pastor, who is a warm and earthy saint, endlessly giving—time, money, charity which has none of the coldness of charity.

She knows the world, but this knowledge has not lowered her great and benevolent dignity; its darkness has not dimmed her goodness.

Immediately on my arrival in Hollywood, a certain American magazine with a huge circulation asked me to write for them a description of the place. But still more important to them was that Miss Monroe and I should be brought face to face, since it was obvious that we were born to hate each other, would do so at first sight, and that our subsequent insults to each other would cause a commotion when reported. They never made a greater mistake.

That afternoon she wore a green dress and, with her yellow hair, looked like a daffodil. We talked mainly, as far as I remember, about Rudolph Steiner, whose works she had just been reading. At one time Helen Rootham was most interested in Steiner, with the result that I found myself, one evening, watching what I believe was known as a Nature-Dance (something uniting one, I expect, with Mother Earth) in which ladies of only too certain an age galloped with large bare dusty feet over an uncarpeted floor. I do not know that this exhibition could be ascribed to Dr. Steiner, but it seemed to have something to do with Higher Thought, and I am afraid that Miss Monroe and I could not resist laughing about it.

In repose her face was at moments strangely, prophetically tragic, like the face of a beautiful ghost—a little spring-ghost, an innocent fertility-daemon, the vegetation spirit that was Ophelia.

Contrasts in Hollywood, apart from the extremes of weather (at one moment a heat wave—which spells to one some strange romance, happy or tragic—at the next moment such raging torrents of rain that one expects, almost, to be drowned standing up), are enormous.

Such are the contrasts between the lives of those who by natural gifts have overcome all obstacles, and the half-death, the misery, of those poor wretches who had been "damned by the rainbow" and who, without talent, had come to Hollywood—misled, perhaps, by the fact that in early youth they had some good looks—to make their fortune, since, they believed, the streets were paved with gold.

On the day on which I first met Miss Monroe, I was brought face to face with these contrasts.

Early on that afternoon I was driven through the rich part of Hollywood to the worst slum in Los Angeles. I forget its real name, but it was known, as all the worst slums in America are known, as "Skid Row."

I was accompanied by the photographers of the magazine that was employing me—kindly, good-humoured men who showed great patience with the poor semi-mad derelicts who wished to be photographed, perhaps in order that, seeing their faces eternalised in this way, they might believe that they were still living.

One of the photographers—and this episode seems to me to give the atmosphere of the lives led by the inhabitants of Hollywood to perfection—had had the strange experience of finding himself at the North Pole one day and, four days afterwards, holding up a violent battle between Red Indians armed with tomahawks in Hollywood; for, having strayed by mistake on to the set, he had succeeded in interposing his head between the rival tomahawks, with the result that he fell flat on his back in a coma, the battle was held up, the whole scene had to be shot again, and he was soundly cursed by the director for his involuntary interference.

My other companion into this Circle of Hell was my coloured maid, Velma (Mrs. LeRoy), who, in 1962, was flown over from Hollywood to appear with me on television, and who has a face like a large yellow hothouse begonia, enormous rolling black eyes, hair which had been straightened but ended at the back in a little black curling drake's tail, and wrists and ankles of an extreme delicacy—amongst the most well-bred I have ever seen. With us, too, was an enormous coloured policeman, a friend of Velma's "dear brothers."

In the wonderful golden weather, we drove, first, into the Chinese quarter, with its fantastic houses painted on the roof with dragons. Here, in spite of the poverty, everyone looked happy. Friendship seemed to be universal. Nothing looked dirty; one could not see any vestiges of despair—perhaps because there had been no ambition; and there were even signs of a humble luxury—fruit shops, for instance, filled with lovely golden, exotic-looking fruits like great moons.

The talk we heard as we drove along the street was like the sound of June leaves drinking rain.

But from Chinatown we emerged into the most appalling slum I have ever seen—worse, even, than those ghastly slums in Naples that no longer exist.

The street was enormously wide. It would take, I think, five minutes to cross it. And that was one of its horrors. For on one pavement a derelict might be dying, friendless, from hunger, and on the other pavement the passing, half-dead creatures would be quite unaware of this, or else, dazed by their own misery, uncaring.

As we emerged from Chinatown we saw, leading out of that monstrous road, on the left, a narrow street going God knows where. Perhaps nowhere, excepting some limbo of Death where all identity would be forgotten.

In spite of the golden weather, that terrible narrow street seemed as if it were enveloped in spangled black gauze. And at the entrance to the street stood a shop that had no windows and no door, and was hung with unspeakable black rags that looked as if they had been stolen from the dead.

There were a number of lodging-houses that looked as if they were inhabited by ghosts and rats only— houses such as that described by James Purdy in his great novella *63: Dream Palace*. And there were numerous missions. These were shaped like coffins, and the derelicts who were utterly starving entered these terrible places and were given a cup of coffee and a doughnut as a reward for listening to a sermon and saying a prayer. There were also horrible-looking music halls, at the entrance to which were enormous bloated figures, grotesquely tall and coarse, dressed as cowboys.

The people who crawled along the pavements looked as if they were made of either red rags or grey rags. Those made up of red rags coughed all the time. The others merely stared.

There is no contact between one human being and another. If you die of starvation, that is *your* affair. You must not expect me, menaced with the same fate, to care. (Every time I see a poor man, I see the Starved Man upon the Cross.)

And what of the homeless beings that drift along that street? I had, at the time when I visited this, been reading Jonathan Swift's *A Modest Proposal*. "I have been assured," he wrote, "that a young healthy well nursed child is at a year old a most delicious, nourishing, and wholesome food. . . . I grant this food will be somewhat dear, and therefore very *proper for Landlords* who, as they have already devoured most of the parents, seem to have the best Title to the children."

There were but few beings who once had been women, and these would have seemed sexless as the dead, had not, once in a while, a child been seen pressed down among the fluttering banners of its misery.

One was anguished as one thought of the plain of winter wolves beneath the hearts of these beings who once had been men and women: no identity . . . no face for tears . . . no memory . . . no years . . . no possessions but the night and day. They once had a name; but now, since there was no one to utter it, they themselves had almost forgotten it. Only their skin showed that they were still living. But after death, as Swift suggested in his *Modest Proposal*, "that Skin, artificially dressed, will make admirable gloves for Ladies, and Summer Boots for Gentlemen."

Blown along the street, they had a special mode of locomotion. In a series of articles on Skid Row, *The Legion of the Damned*, that appeared in the *Mirror* of Los Angeles, Mr. Lou Larkin, who had spent ten days in the Row, said of these poor derelicts: "They don't walk. They keep falling forward. It is a slow muscleless movement dependent almost entirely on the law of gravity . . . the torso is allowed to fall forward, the right knee joint locks, supporting the body, which then rocks slightly to the right. This movement lifts the left leg from the ground. Free, it swings forward another twenty inches and so on. Veteran bums will tell you that this mode of locomotion requires less energy than standing in one place." If you should ask them where they are going, how should they know? Coming from nowhere and going nowhere—like everything and everybody else. Wishing only that the world would end.

But, looking at these beings, I thought:
"Perhaps it *has* ended."

* * *

I had seen Skid Row gilded by a false spring light. But now, in my sleepless nights, I walk through that long street again, ungilded by that light, but as it exists in reality, in a world fallen into winter. And I was a part of that winter world.

Winter is the time for comfort, for good food and warmth, for the touch of a friendly hand and for a talk beside the fire: it is the time for home. It is no season in which to wander the world as if one were the wind, blowing aimlessly along the streets without a place in which to rest, without food and without time meaning anything to one, just as time means nothing to the wind. All that means anything to the wind is beginning and ending. And coldness. But here, in the city's circles of Hell, sunk beneath the world-height of empty houses, twenty thousand persons creep who have neither friend nor shelter. All through the day, under the Bedlam daylight's murderous roar, changing to the enormous Tartarean darkness of a fog, through these deepest circles of Hell all forms of misery loomed and faded, monstrous shapes, their sightless faces turned to the unheeding sky, tapping upon the ground with a hollow noise that seemed to echo down millions of fathoms to the very centre of the ball of the earth. For in this city of universal night, only the blind can see. Along the wide pavements that were long and hard as Hell's huge polar street, cold as the universal blackness of Hell's day, the towers of rags and bones were swept—each a universe of misery, a world of hunger and polar wastes, shut off from all others. Some were young, and these had nothing between their one outer covering of rags and their skin, so that it seemed they had early been made ready for the grave. With those who were older, it was as if all the nations of the dead, with their million-year-old rags about them, had risen to denounce us. A whisper would pierce my sleeplessness. "What have we done? What have we done? Now it is always night, and winter. And we have been thrown down into Hell. Night after night! Week after week, month after month, year after year. . . . How many moments go to an hour, how many hours go to a night, how many nights go to a year, how many years go to a life? And every night an eternity of cold."

"Why don't they bury us?" another voice said. "Oh, why don't they bury us? It'd be warmer there."

Outside my house there is still a little flurry of dust, the chatter of the people who still hope to intrude on me and rot my brain, as they have tried to do throughout my life.

But all is more silent now, a shrunken world of no horizons. Yet sometimes I see a giant lion-paw on my window sill, and my three Visitors still come: Her with the one tooth (but what a grinding wolf's tooth that would be were there something to bite upon instead of just emptiness!) —Her with the one eye, looking into the

229

bleak future, with the blind fumes from the Bomb enclosing it—Her with the one ear, waiting for some message from the Beyond.

These, the three Norns, still visit me. But soon they will cease to do so.

Then all will be over, bar the shouting and the worms.

Index

Edith Sitwell

Edith Louisa Sitwell was born on September 7, 1887, at Scarborough, England, the only daughter and eldest child of Sir George Reresby Sitwell, fourth baronet, and Lady Ida Emily Augusta Denison, daughter of the Earl of Londesborough.

She grew up at Renishaw, the Sitwell estate near Sheffield which had been in the family for six hundred years, and was educated by governesses. Just before the First World War she moved to London, where she readily established a salon and, in 1915, published her first collection of verse, *The Mother and Other Poems*. She attracted public attention in 1916 when she edited *Wheels*, the first of six annual anthologies which served as a platform for young poets and to which she and her brothers, Osbert and Sacheverell, were the chief contributors.

Dame Edith's recitation through a megaphone of her entertainment in verse, *Façade*, accompanied by the music of Sir William Walton, took place at the Aeolian Hall in London on June 12, 1923, and met with savage critical reaction. The American première of the same cycle of poems took place at the Museum of Modern Art in New York City on January 28, 1949.

Through the years she published an impressive amount of poetry and of non-fiction, although for some years after the appearance in 1930 of her biography of Alexander Pope she wrote very little.

After her *Collected Poems* appeared in 1954, she published two additional volumes of verse: *The Outcasts* and *Music and Ceremonies*. Notable among her non-fiction are *The Queens and the Hive, Fanfare for Elizabeth, English Eccentrics* and *A Poet's Notebook*. She also edited *The Atlantic Book of British and American Poetry* and other anthologies.

In 1933 she received for her poetry a medal of the Royal Society of Literature, and was later made vice president and one of the ten Companions of that society. In 1954 she was created a Dame Commander of the Order of the British Empire by Queen Elizabeth II. She held honorary literary doctorates from Leeds, Durham, Oxford and Sheffield universities, and was an honorary associate of the American National Institute of Arts and Letters.

Dame Edith made many trips to America and to the Continent, and lived in Paris for several years. She never married.

In 1955 she was received into the Roman Catholic Church. In 1962 her seventy-fifth birthday was celebrated in England with the reissue of several of her books and with a concert in which Sir William Walton took part.

During the last years of her life Dame Edith lived in the Hampstead district of London. She died of heart failure on December 9, 1964, in London, after having been admitted earlier in the day to St. Thomas Hospital. She was 77 years old.